Drucker

A Life in Pictures

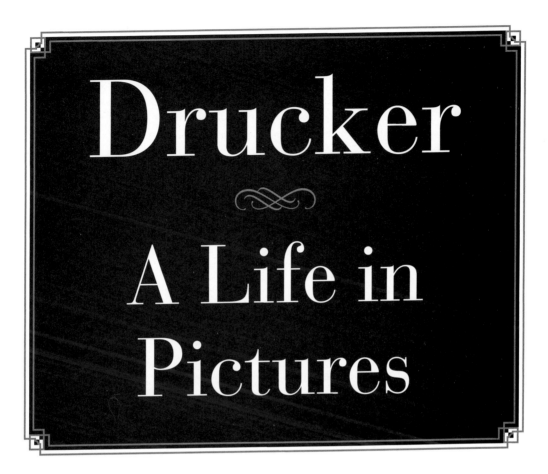

Drucker

A Life in Pictures

Rick Wartzman
Photographs by Anne Fishbein
Curated by Bridget Lawlor

NEW YORK   CHICAGO   SAN FRANCISCO
LISBON   LONDON   MADRID   MEXICO CITY   MILAN
NEW DELHI   SAN JUAN   SEOUL   SINGAPORE
SYDNEY   TORONTO

The **McGraw·Hill** Companies

1 2 3 4 5 6 7 8 9 0   QFR/QFR   1 8 7 6 5 4 3 2

ISBN   978-0-07-170046-7
MHID   0-07-170046-3

e-ISBN 978-0-07-176308-0
e-MHID   0-07-176308-2

Design by Mauna Eichner and Lee Fukui

McGraw-Hill books are available at special quantity discounts to use as premiums and sales promotions or for use in corporate training programs. To contact a representative, please e-mail us at bulksales@mcgraw-hill.com.

This book is printed on acid-free paper.

Library of Congress Cataloging-in-Publication Data

Wartzman, Rick.
  Drucker : a life in pictures / by Rick Wartzman.
    p. cm.
  ISBN 978-0-07-170046-7 (alk. paper) — ISBN 0-07-170046-3 (alk. paper)
1. Drucker, Peter F. (Peter Ferdinand), 1909-2005. 2. Social scientists—United States—Biography. 3. Business consultants—United States--Biography. I. Title.
  H59.D75W37 2013
  300'.92--dc23
  [B]
                                                                2012034109

Contents

Introduction

Peter Drucker always relished his place as an outsider, or, as he liked to put it, "a bystander."

"Bystanders have no history of their own," he wrote. "They are on the stage but not part of the action. They are not even audience. The fortunes of the play and of every actor in it depend on the audience whereas the reaction of the bystander has no effect except on himself. But standing in the wings—much like the fireman in the theater—the bystander sees things neither actor nor audience notices. Above all, he sees differently from the way actors or audience see. Bystanders reflect—and reflection is a prism rather than a mirror; it refracts."

No one would dispute that Drucker possessed incredible powers of observation. With an ability, as he described it, to "look out the window and see what's visible but not yet seen," Drucker discerned some of the major trends and events of the twentieth century before almost anyone else spotted them: the Hitler-Stalin pact, Japan's impending rise to economic power, the shift from manufacturing to knowledge work, the increasing importance of the service sector, the fall of the Soviet Union. "Peter Drucker's eyeballs," Harvard University's Rosabeth Moss Kanter once marveled, "must contain crystal balls."

But for Drucker to have suggested that he was merely a bystander was hardly accurate. He didn't just stand in the wings. For 70 years, he was very much in the play. Often, he was its star. Or the director. Or the playwright. Or all three at once.

The pages that follow—featuring photographs of items from the Drucker Archives, part of the Drucker Institute at Claremont Graduate University—are meant to shine a spotlight on Drucker in a variety of roles. Among them are an immigrant fleeing the Nazis in the 1930s; a teacher; a writer (whose enormous body of work, as the *Atlantic*'s Jack Beatty has asserted, has arguably had "more influence for the good" than anyone else's in the last 50 years); a consultant to corporations, nonprofits, and government agencies the world over; and a family man and friend.

Indeed, I have tried to write the captions accompanying the images in this book as a narrative that captures many of the most salient themes and episodes from Drucker's life. Interlaced throughout the book, meanwhile, are excerpts from various interviews that Drucker gave over the years.

Drucker also loved to ask questions of others, and among his most pointed was surely this: "What do you want to be remembered for?" As this book makes clear, Drucker will long be remembered for the huge positive impact he had on the way our institutions are managed and, in turn, the shape of our society.

That said, this is not intended to be a definitive biography in pictures. Unfortunately, the Drucker Archives doesn't have a comprehensive enough collection to even attempt such a thing. It is Drucker himself who is mostly to blame for this deficiency. Simply put, he wasn't much of a pack rat.

I don't know why Drucker didn't save more of his letters and other papers; one can only imagine the rich history that got tossed away when Drucker discarded correspondence with legendary General Motors Chairman Alfred Sloan or inventor-philosopher R. Buckminster Fuller or communications theorist Marshall McLuhan. He was close with all of them—and so many more.

I can only speculate that Drucker had two reasons for not hanging on to more remnants from times gone by. The first is that, while he was certainly a student of the past, Drucker was firmly focused on the future. "It is not possible to create tomorrow," he advised organizations, "unless one first sloughs off yesterday." Second, there's a measure of vanity in filing things away for posterity. And Drucker, by all accounts, was a man without much ego.

Nonetheless, the Drucker Archives has plenty of material—more than 10,000 documents, photographs, videos, awards, and realia—to tell a good story about an extraordinary person. The archives was formally launched in 1998, seven years before Drucker's death at the age of 95. But it began unofficially sometime before that when Bob Buford, a dear friend of Drucker's (who now serves as chairman emeritus of the Drucker Institute), made a very wise capital investment: he bought a few cardboard boxes and started fishing stuff out of Drucker's garage before it began to molder, or, as he says, "the mice could eat it." In more recent years, Drucker's widow, Doris, has continued to add items to the archives as she finds things around the house.

Most significant, the archives has become much more aggressive of late in searching for Drucker artifacts in other repositories across the country and around the globe; many of these new discoveries are shown here. This proactive approach is thanks to the brains and passion of our archivist, Bridget Lawlor, who joined the institute staff in the summer of 2009 and cocurated this book with me.

The other member of our team was Anne Fishbein, whose wonderful photography graces these pages. She's a remarkable talent, as evidenced by those that hold or have exhibited her pictures: the Art Institute of Chicago, the Los Angeles County Museum of Art, the Museum of Modern Art in New York, and the San Francisco Museum of Fine Art, among others.

The three of us—Bridget, Anne, and I—have thoroughly enjoyed putting together this project. Along the way, as he always does, Peter Drucker gave us new ways to think about our own work and our own lives. We trust he'll do the same for you.

Rick Wartzman
Claremont, California

Drucker

A Life in
Pictures

Peter Drucker in the 1930s

The
Immigrant

Peter Drucker: You want to know my story? I became a journalist on my twentieth birthday. Foreign and business editor of the second-largest afternoon paper in Europe, and I reported for work on January 2nd.

I had been a trainee in a cotton export house and a trainee in an investment bank. I had never been in a newspaper. . . . It's a morning paper and afternoon paper, so we went to work at 6 in the morning. And I took the first streetcar on the 2nd of January in Frankfurt. . . . And that streetcar stopped outside that newspaper building at three minutes past 6. I went up the three stairs so I was up there at six minutes past 6. And there stood the editor-in-chief . . . and he said, "Young man, if you're here tomorrow at five minutes past 6, you don't have to come in." And I said, "The only streetcar—the first streetcar—starts at 5:28." Whereupon he took the telephone . . . and woke up the mayor of Frankfurt, and the next day the streetcar line started at five minutes past 5, and I was on it.

The Austrian household in which Peter Drucker grew up was one of great intellectual ferment. His parents, Adolph and Caroline, regularly held evening salons with economists (including Joseph Schumpeter, who would come to have a tremendous influence on Drucker), politicians, musicians, writers, and scientists. "That was actually my education," Drucker later said. Pictured here are Drucker's baptismal certificate and a crystal goblet given to the Drucker family to mark the occasion of Peter's birth, November 19, 1909.

Tauf-Schein.

Auszug aus dem Taufbuche der evangel. Pfarrgemeinde Augsb. Bekenntn. in

Jahr *1909.* Zahl *180.*

Name des Täufenden	Zeit (Jahr, Monat, Tag)		Ort		Geschlecht			
					männlich		weiblich	
	der Geburt	der Taufe	der Geburt (Haus-Nr.)	der Taufe	ehelich	unehelich	ehelich	unehelich
Johann	Eintausend neun hundert neun un neunzehn 19. November 1909	24. Dezember	Wien XIX Döblinger Haupt- straße 42	Wien	1			

Name des Täuflings:

Peter Georg Ferdinand Drucker

Eltern des Täuflings:		Taufpaten
Vater	Mutter	
Dr. jur. Adolf Drucker bb Sekretär des öst. Handel Bankund ... Professor in der Universität	Caroline geborne Bondi aus Wien	Maria Lang II Kleguheimagt. 12
		Hebamme: Anna Winter

Urkund dessen die amtliche Fertigung.

Pfarramt der evangel. Gemeinde Augsb. Bekenntn.

Wien, a... PFARRAMT A. B. 17. JUN. 1910

Drucker was born into a country whose power was about to be shattered by the onset of World War I; his native Vienna was soon to be "rendered a mere capital of nostalgia," as Drucker biographer Jack Beatty put it. Recalled Drucker: "I was surrounded by extinct volcanoes." For a young man who was focused on the future, it was time to move on. Seen here are a proclamation given to Drucker's father for his service in the Austrian Ministry of Economics and a 1984 letter in which Drucker reminisced about his days in the Gymnasium in Vienna and the antics of two troublemakers in his class.

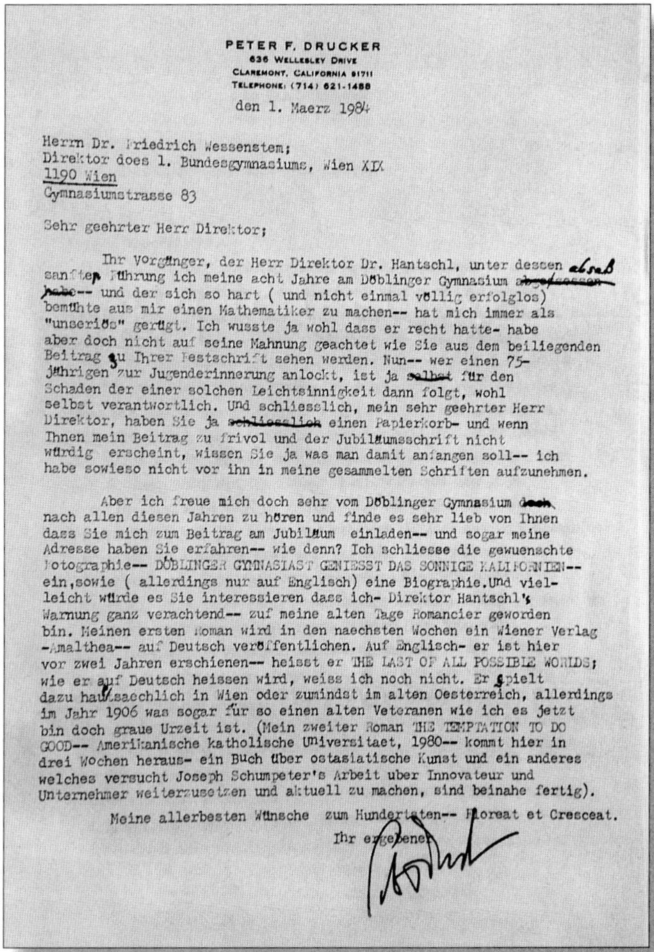

PETER F. DRUCKER
636 WELLESLEY DRIVE
CLAREMONT, CALIFORNIA 91711
TELEPHONE: (714) 621-1488

den 1. Maerz 1984

Herrn Dr. Friedrich Wessenstem;
Direktor does 1. Bundesgymnasiums, Wien XIX
1190 Wien
Gymnasiumstrasse 83

Sehr geehrter Herr Direktor;

Ihr Vorgänger, der Herr Direktor Dr. Hantschl, unter dessen absaß sanften Führung ich meine acht Jahre am Döblinger Gymnasium ~~abgesessen habe~~-- und der sich so hart (und nicht einmal völlig erfolglos) bemühte aus mir einen Mathematiker zu machen-- hat mich immer als "unseriös" gerügt. Ich wusste ja wohl dass er recht hatte- habe aber doch nicht auf seine Mahnung geachtet wie Sie aus dem beiliegenden Beitrag zu Ihrer Festschrift sehen werden. Nun-- wer einen 75-jährigen zur Jugenderinnerung anlockt, ist ja ~~selbst~~ für den Schaden der einer solchen Leichtsinnigkeit dann folgt, wohl selbst verantwortlich. Und schliesslich, mein sehr geehrter Herr Direktor, haben Sie ja ~~schliesslich~~ einen Papierkorb- und wenn Ihnen mein Beitrag zu frivol und der Jubiläumsschrift nicht würdig erscheint, wissen Sie ja was man damit anfangen soll-- ich habe sowieso nicht vor ihn in meine gesammelten Schriften aufzunehmen.

Aber ich freue mich doch sehr vom Döblinger Gymnasium ~~doch~~ nach allen diesen Jahren zu hören und finde es sehr lieb von Ihnen dass Sie mich zum Beitrag am Jubiläum einladen-- und sogar meine Adresse haben Sie erfahren-- wie denn? Ich schliesse die gewuenschte Fotographie-- DÖBLINGER GYMNASIAST GENIESST DAS SONNIGE KALIFORNIEN-- ein,sowie (allerdings nur auf Englisch) eine Biographie.Und vielleicht würde es Sie interessieren dass ich- Direktor Hantschl's Warnung ganz verachtend-- auf meine alten Tage Romancier geworden bin. Meinen ersten Roman wird in den naechsten Wochen ein Wiener Verlag -Amalthea-- auf Deutsch veröffentlichen. Auf Englisch- er ist hier vor zwei Jahren erschienen-- heisst er THE LAST OF ALL POSSIBLE WORLDS; wie er auf Deutsch heissen wird, weiss ich noch nicht. Er spielt dazu hauptsaechlich in Wien oder zumindst im alten Oesterreich, allerdings im Jahr 1906 was sogar für so einen alten Veteranen wie ich es jetzt bin doch graue Urzeit ist. (Mein zweiter Roman THE TEMPTATION TO DO GOOD-- Amerikanische katholische Universitaet, 1980-- kommt hier in drei Wochen heraus- ein Buch über ostasiatische Kunst und ein anderes welches versucht Joseph Schumpeter's Arbeit uber Innovateur und Unternehmer weiterzusetzen und aktuell zu machen, sind beinahe fertig).

Meine allerbesten Wünsche zum Hundertjaten-- Floreat et Cresceat.

Ihr ergebener

At age 17, Drucker left Vienna to work at an export firm in Hamburg, Germany. His father was not pleased. "He . . . wanted me to be a full-time university student," Drucker said, "but I was tired of being a schoolboy and wanted to go to work." Eventually, Drucker studied at Hamburg University and then earned his doctorate at Frankfurt University. Shown here is Drucker's student identification card, along with his 1932 doctoral dissertation, "The Justification of International Law and the Will of the State."

When Drucker set off for Hamburg, his parents had the hat and coat and tails pictured here made for him. They thought that an up-and-coming young man like Peter would surely make good use of such formal wear at various social functions. In reality, however, Drucker didn't get out much. Even though he had gotten to know well one of the city's "respected patrician families," Drucker later recalled "living in Hamburg by myself on a clerk trainee's stipend," which was "inadequate to get by in the most modest style."

Ehn.A.-   24.April 1933.

Herrn Dr. Peter D r u c k e r

                Frankfurt a.M.

                Schillerstr.19/25

Sehr verehrter Herr Doktor, in der Anlage erlaube
        ich mir, Ihnen den Entwurf einer Liste zu
        übersenden, nach der ich die Rezensionsexem-
        plare Ihrer Schrift über Friedrich Julius
        Stahl, zu verschicken gedenke. Ich möchte
        Sie höflichst bitten, mir diese Liste mit
        Ihren evlt.Wünschen für irgendwelche Aende-
        rungen und Ergänzungen umgehend zurücksen-
        den zu wollen, da die Versendung noch im
        Laufe dieser Woche erfolgen soll.
            Gleichzeitig darf ich Sie bitten, freund-
        lichst über die Ihnen lt.unseren Verlagsver-
        trag zustehenden Freiexemplare verfügen zu
        wollen.
            In vorzüglicher Hochachtung Ihr ergebenst

In 1932, Drucker told a friend, "If the Nazis come to power, I shan't stay in Germany." Never, though, would he forget the Nazis' ascent. Watching society's institutions crumble led Drucker to conclude that "performing, responsible management is the alternative to tyranny." Seen here is a letter to Drucker from German publisher Paul Siebeck, who put out a Drucker monograph on philosopher Friedrich Julius Stahl. The Nazis burned it. They did the same with Drucker's *The Jewish Question in Germany*, also pictured here. In 1933, Drucker left Germany for England.

Dr. Peter Drucker.   OPINION.

Professor Mendelsohn-Bartholdy says that he has made enquiries

and that nobody at Frankfurt has heard of Drucker.

                          C. M. S.

In 1934, as seen here, Drucker applied for a program to help
"displaced German scholars" land U.S. academic positions. He
was rejected. Why? "Nobody at Frankfurt has heard of Drucker."
That didn't stop him from going on to a hugely successful career
as a writer and teacher. But even in these things, Austria had left
him ill equipped in one way. As he noted in a 1985 letter to the
writer Irving Kristol, also shown here: "I am the only person in
the history of Austrian education . . . who managed to flunk the
elective typing course in my Gymnasium."

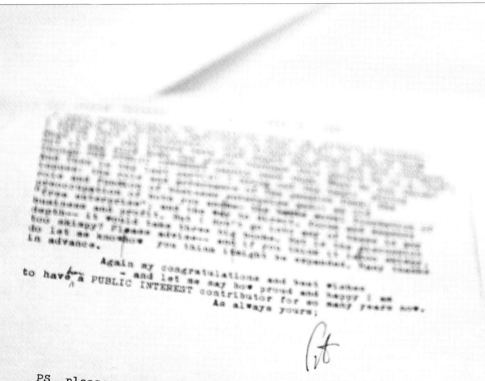

Again my congratulations and best wishes
— and let me say how proud and happy I am
to have a PUBLIC INTEREST contributor for so many years now.
As always yours:

PS please excuse my typing-- tis but a poor thing but mine
own. I am up in the mountains and without a secretary-- and
I am the only person in the history of Austrian education, both
before me and since- who managed to flunk the elective typing
course in my Gymnasium. But also this is a brand-new typewriter;
we bought it the day before we left California to drive up here
and yours is the first letter I've typed on it.

In 1937, Drucker and his wife of three years, Doris, immigrated to the United States, where he wrote for a number of European newspapers. He never looked back. Asked at the end of his life what it felt like to be under the rule of another Austrian, California governor Arnold Schwarzenegger, Drucker replied dryly: "I'm not impressed with Austrians. I've known too many of them." Shown here are the ship manifest from the Druckers' voyage to New York and Peter's U.S. citizenship card.

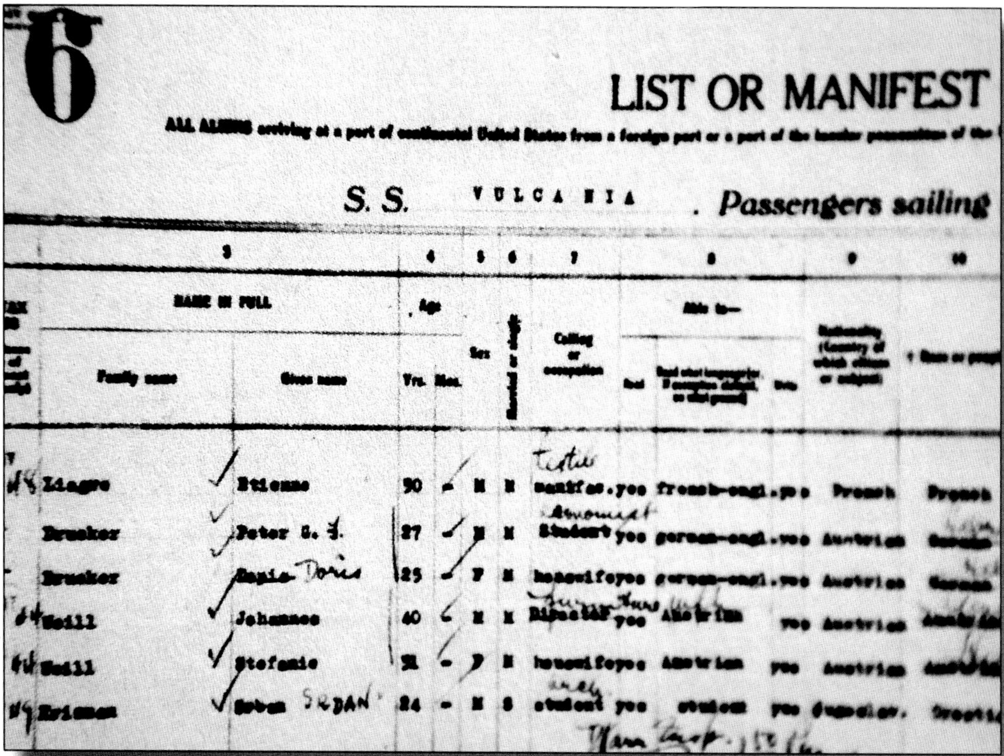
6

LIST OR MANIFEST

S. S. VULCANIA . Passengers sailing

Family name	Given name	Yrs.	Sex	Calling or occupation
Ziagro	Etienne	30	M	
Drucker	Peter F. J.	27	M	Student
Drucker	Doris	25	F	housewife
Weill	Johannes	40	M	
Weill	Stefanie		F	housewife
		24	M	student

No. 5325845

Name BECKER Peter Ferdinand
  Bronxville,
residing at 19 Bayberry St., Bronxville Kent, New Y

Age 38 years. Date of order of admission July 29 29th, 19

Date certificate issued July 29th, 1943 by the

U.S. District Court at New York City, New York

Petition No. 402 967

x Peter Ferdinand Becker
(Complete and true signature of holder)

Peter Drucker signs his books

The
Writer

Interviewer: If you describe your occupation, would it be "writer"?

Peter Drucker: I always say I write.

Interviewer: What, then, has inspired your books more than anything?

PD: The same thing that inspires tuberculosis. This is a serious, degenerative, compulsive disorder and addiction.

Interviewer: An addiction to writing?

PD: To writing, yes.

DR. PETER F. DRUCKER

Economist • Financial Correspondent • International Trade Consultant • Author and Lecturer

Author of
"THE END OF ECONOMIC MAN"
"GERMANY, THE LAST FOUR YEARS"

Contributor to
"JOURNAL OF COMMERCE" • **"HARPERS"**
"THE NEW REPUBLIC" • **"WASHINGTON POST"**
"ASIA" • **"VIRGINIAN QUARTERLY REVIEW"**

American financial correspondent for
"THE FINANCIAL NEWS OF LONDON"
"THE GLASGOW HERALD"
and other British papers

FOR a penetrating analysis of the economic forces at work in the world today, affecting markets and standards of living in every land, there is probably no better informed speaker and writer living in America today than Dr. Peter F. Drucker. Leading American and British investment houses whom he serves as a confidential staff consultant on international trade, say that he is "one expert with his feet on the ground."

Dr. Drucker witnessed Germany's financial collapse under its pre-Hitler leaders and knows the utter despair that it brought to all classes, making the rise of Nazism possible. He knows, too, the full potency of its insidious appeal to the proletariat of other countries. While condemning both Communism and Fascism, Dr. Drucker contends that capitalistic society has as much to fear from Fascism as from Communism.

His new book, "The End of Economic Man," is being hailed by economists everywhere as the most thought-provoking analysis of the totalitarian ideology that has yet appeared and one that is fraught with the utmost significance for those who would preserve the democratic ideal in our own land.

Raymond Leslie Buell, president of the Foreign Policy Association and one of the editors of Fortune Magazine, calls it "the most penetrating analysis of Fascist economics that I have seen and, indeed the most acute criticism of the conflict of present day ideologies." H. N. Brailsford, the distinguished British economist, who writes the highly laudatory introduction, declares that "to us all his book is a summons. The end of Economic Man forces on us a revaluation of our values."

Though keenly alert to the philosophic concepts and social implications of his material, Dr. Drucker's lectures are practical in nature, designed to help business men to better understand those forces in their own business over which they themselves have no control. They are presented in terms that the average business man can understand and appreciate.

To his profoundly stimulating and highly informative lectures Dr. Drucker brings an extraordinarily diversified and thorough training. Born in Vienna in 1907 of an upper bourgeoisie family prominently identified with pre-war Austrian governmental affairs, he was educated at the Universities of Hamburg and Frankfurt in Germany and did post graduate study at Cambridge University in England. As financial editor of the once powerful Frankfurter General Anzeiger and consultant for leading German and more recently, English business interests, he has roved Europe, the Near East, Africa and South America investigating potential markets and studying economic conditions generally.

Exclusive Management: W. COLSTON LEIGH, Inc.

Drucker hadn't been in America very long before he won fame as a writer. His first major work, 1939's *The End of Economic Man*, explored the rise of fascism in Europe. The book earned praise from Winston Churchill and made Drucker a sought-after speaker. Pictured here is a 1940s poster touting a series of lectures delivered by Drucker. Also shown are the original acknowledgments for Drucker's 1973 magnum opus, *Management: Tasks, Responsibilities, Practices*. They underscore a central Drucker tenet: that ideas must be turned into action.

of today and tomorrow. It tries to develop at least fundamental approaches

to knowledge that goes way beyond what we possess so far.

But above all, the purpose of the two books is quite different.

The purpose of "The Practice of Management" was to make managers

think about management. It is to make them aware of their function

and their importance. This of course is also one aim of the present book.

Peter F. Drucker   200/5

But above all the present book aims at motivating managers to act.

The focus of the present book is not on knowledge alone. It is on

performance and responsibility.

          *   *   *

Perhaps the most amazing thing about *Management:Tasks, Responsibilities,Practices* (aside from its sheer heft, at more than 800 pages) was its stunning popularity; the tome topped *The Joy of Sex* on the national bestseller list. Drucker had clearly come a long way since his earlier days, when he wrote for more obscure publications. Shown here is the table of contents for *Management* that Drucker sent to his publisher. Also pictured is a 1940 letter to the *Virginia Quarterly Review*, which Drucker credited for "my literary start in this country."

```
                            Contents/1

PETER F. DRUCKER                          MANAGEMENT

              TABLE OF CONTENTS

                                              page numbers

           PREFACE: THE ALTERNATIVE TO TYRANNY      I to XIV

              INTRODUCTION: FROM "MANAGEMENT BOOM
                            TO MANAGEMENT PERFORMANCE    1/0

    Ch. 1  The Emergence of Management              1/1 -- 1/31

    Ch. 2  The Management Boom and its lessons      2/1 -- 2/66

    Ch. 3  New Challenges                           3/1-3/23


              .PART ONE  THE TASKS                     4/0

      Ch. 4  The Dimensions of Management           4/1 -- 4/34
      XEKXXEX
Business Performance                               5/0
      Ch. 5  Managing a Business: The Sears Story   5/1--5/23
      Ch. 6  What is a Business?                    6/1--6/54
      Ch. 7  Business Purpose and Business Mission  7/1--7/79
      Ch. 8  The Power & Purpose of Objectives: The
             Marks & Spencer Story                  8/1-8/27
      Ch. 9  Strategies, Objectives, Priorities &
             Work Assignments                       9/1--9/59
      Ch. 10 Strategic Planning: The Entrepeneurial Skill  10/1 --10/29

Performance in the Service Institution
                                                   11/0
      Ch. 11 The Multi-Institutional Society        11/1-- 11/20
      Ch. 12 Why Service Institutions do not perform  12/1--12/41
      Ch. 13 Managing Service Institutions for Performance  13/1-13/69
```

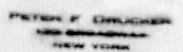

PETER F. DRUCKER

NEW YORK

98 Liberty Street
September 19, 1940

Archibald B. Shepperson, Esq.,
THE VIRGINIA QUARTERLY REVIEW,
Charlottesville, Virginia.

My dear Mr. Shepperson:

I would be only too happy to have an article of
mine in THE VIRGINIA QUARTERLY; not only because I owe to
you my literary start in this country but also because I
feel that it is a great honor for anyone to be allowed to
write for the Quarterly.

Unfortunately, neither of the two pieces you sug
gest seem to me feasible. As to my address before the
Institute of Public Affairs, the "Analist" has reprinted
that with permission from the Institute; and as to the
Balkans I do not feel brave enough to make forecasts at
But there is one subject which might interest you and w
would come in handy from my point of view. This is a d
question of the fundamental changes inside the German s
starting from the fact that up till quite recently we
people pinned their hope for internal revolution to t
upon the army. I would like to show why the "Prussia
and the conditions on which comparatively limited and
to carry out stunned such high hope. This will become

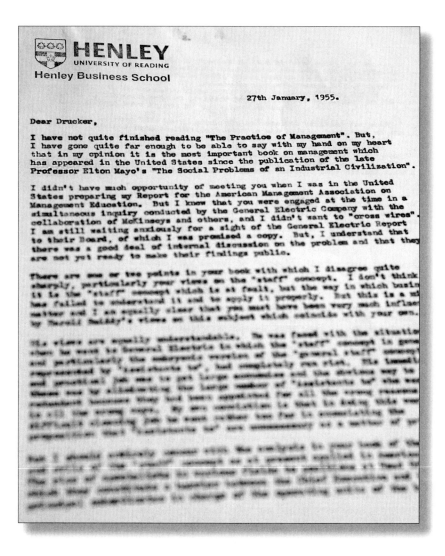

HENLEY
UNIVERSITY OF READING
Henley Business School

27th January, 1955.

Dear Drucker,

I have not quite finished reading "The Practice of Management". But, I have gone quite far enough to be able to say with my hand on my heart that in my opinion it is the most important book on management which has appeared in the United States since the publication of the late Professor Elton Mayo's "The Social Problems of an Industrial Civilization".

I didn't have much opportunity of meeting you when I was in the United States preparing my Report for the American Management Association on Management Education. But I knew that you were engaged at the time in a simultaneous inquiry conducted by the General Electric Company with the collaboration of McKinseys and others, and I didn't want to "cross wires". I am still waiting anxiously for a sight of the General Electric Report to their Board, of which I was promised a copy. But, I understand that there was a good deal of internal discussion on the problem and that they are not yet ready to make their findings public.

There are one or two points in your book with which I disagree quite sharply, particularly your views on the "staff" concept. I don't think it is the "staff" concept which is at fault, but the way in which busin[ess] has failed to understand it and to apply it properly. But this is a m[inor] matter and I am equally clear that you must have been very much influen[ced] by Harold Smiddy's views on this subject which coincide with your own.

His views are equally understandable. He was faced with the situati[on] when he went to General Electric in which the "staff" concept in gene[ral] and particularly the embryonic version of the "general staff" concept represented by "assistants to", had completely run riot. His immedi[ate] and practical job was to get large economies and the obvious way to [do] them was by eliminating the large number of "assistants to" who wer[e] employed because they had been appointed for all the wrong reasons [and] to all the wrong ends. My conclusion is that in doing this you [have] difficult dancing jab he went rather too far in condemning the difficult dancing jab he went rather too far in condemning the [...] proposition that "assistants to" are unnecessary as a matter of pr[...]

But I should entirely agree with the analysis in your book of the [...] use of the "staff" concept as at present applied in American [...] the view of centralizing to nucleus limits by services at least to [...] which they constitute a burden between the chief Executive and [...] which they constitute a burden in charge of the operating units of the [...]

When Drucker set out to write *The Practice of Management*, he was, as he would later describe it, "very conscious of the fact that I was laying the foundations of a discipline." Shown here is a 1955 letter from management theorist Lyndall Urwick, who called the book "the most important" in the field since Elton Mayo's *The Social Problems of an Industrial Civilization*. Chances are that Drucker would have frowned on such a comparison. He loathed Mayo, whom he branded in a 1985 letter, also shown here, as "lazy, autocratic and a boor."

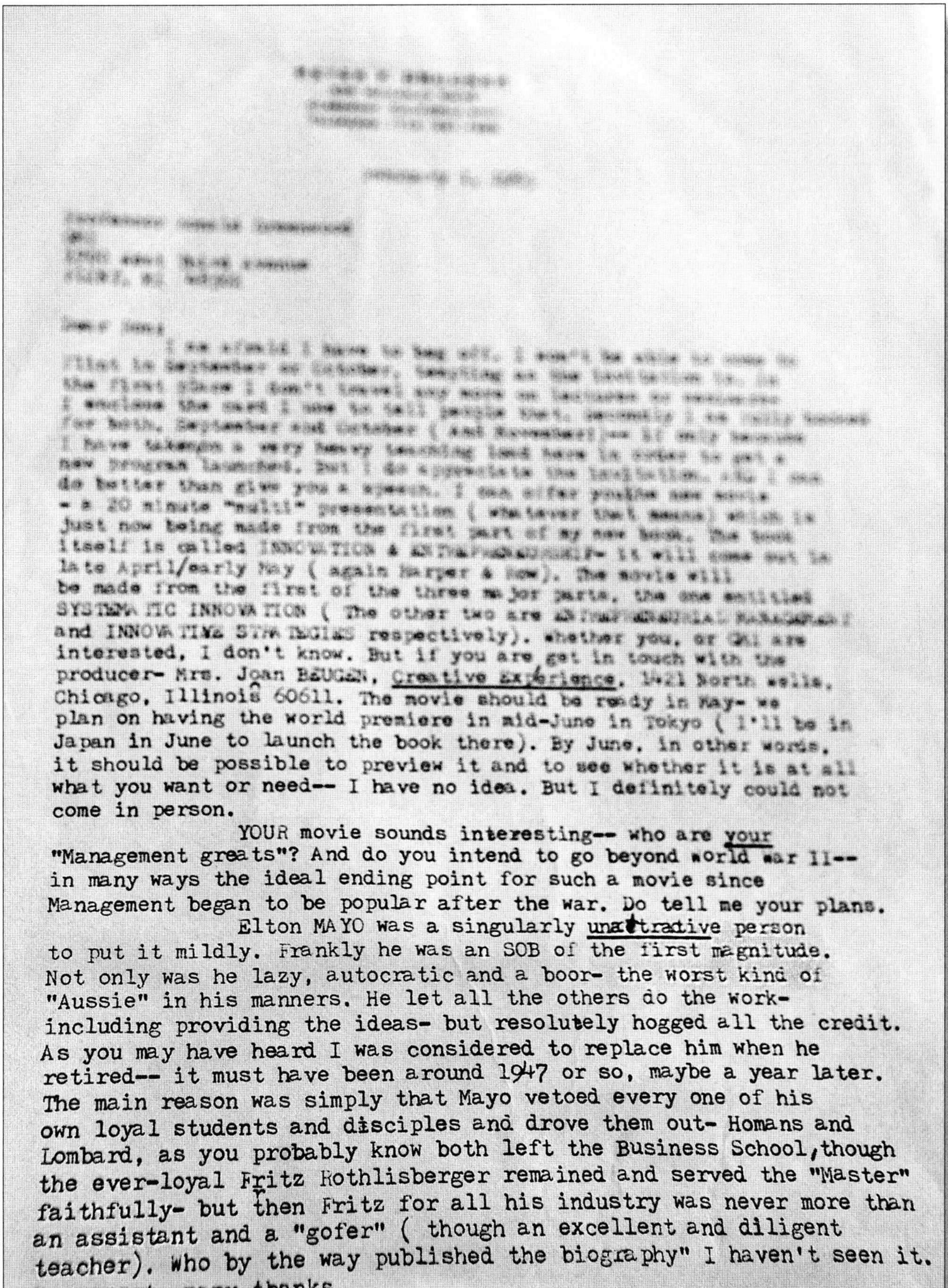

[letterhead illegible]

[date illegible]

[address illegible]

Dear Doug

I am afraid I have to beg off. I won't be able to come to
Flint in September or October, tempting as the invitation is. In
the first place I don't travel any more on business or [illegible]
I enclose the card I use to tell people that, secondly I am fully booked
for both, September and October (And November)-- as if only because
I have taken on a very heavy teaching load here in order to get a
new program launched. But I do appreciate the invitation. Why I can
do better than give you a speech. I can offer you the same movie
- a 20 minute "multi" presentation (whatever that means) which is
just now being made from the first part of my new book. The book
itself is called INNOVATION & ENTREPRENEURSHIP- it will come out in
late April/early May (again Harper & Row). The movie will
be made from the first of the three major parts, the one entitled
SYSTEMATIC INNOVATION (The other two are ENTREPRENEURIAL MANAGEMENT
and INNOVATIVE STRATEGIES respectively). Whether you, or GMI are
interested, I don't know. But if you are get in touch with the
producer- Mrs. Joan BEUGEN, Creative Experience, 1421 North Wells,
Chicago, Illinois 60611. The movie should be ready in May- we
plan on having the world premiere in mid-June in Tokyo (I'll be in
Japan in June to launch the book there). By June, in other words,
it should be possible to preview it and to see whether it is at all
what you want or need-- I have no idea. But I definitely could not
come in person.

     YOUR movie sounds interesting-- who are your
"Management greats"? And do you intend to go beyond world war ll--
in many ways the ideal ending point for such a movie since
Management began to be popular after the war. Do tell me your plans.

     Elton MAYO was a singularly unattractive person
to put it mildly. Frankly he was an SOB of the first magnitude.
Not only was he lazy, autocratic and a boor- the worst kind of
"Aussie" in his manners. He let all the others do the work-
including providing the ideas- but resolutely hogged all the credit.
As you may have heard I was considered to replace him when he
retired-- it must have been around 1947 or so, maybe a year later.
The main reason was simply that Mayo vetoed every one of his
own loyal students and disciples and drove them out- Homans and
Lombard, as you probably know both left the Business School,though
the ever-loyal Fritz Rothlisberger remained and served the "Master"
faithfully- but then Fritz for all his industry was never more than
an assistant and a "gofer" (though an excellent and diligent
teacher). Who by the way published the biography" I haven't seen it.
Do report- many thanks.

The Writer

29

ドラッカー博士　著作一覧

① *Friedrich Julius Stahl, Konservative Staatslehre und Geshichtliche Entwicklung.* Tuebingen: Mohr, 1933.（本邦未訳）

② *The End of Economic Man.* John Day, 1939.（Reprint by Harper & Row, 1969.）（岩根忠訳「経済人の終わり」東洋経済新報社、昭和38。）

③ *The Future of Industrial Man.* John Day, 1942.（岩根忠訳「産業にたずさわる人の未来」東洋経済新報社、昭和39；田代義範訳「産業人の未来」未来社、昭和40。）

④ *Concept of the Corporation.* John Day, 1946.（Reprint by John Day, 1972.）（岩根忠訳「会社という概念」東洋経済新報社、昭和41；下川浩一訳「現代大企業論」上・下、未来社、昭和41。）

⑤ *The New Society.* Harper & Row, 1950.（現代経営研究会訳「新しい社会と新しい経営」ダイヤモンド社、昭和32。）

⑥ *The Practice of Management.* Harper & Row, 1954.（野田一夫監修、現代経営研究会訳「現代の経営」正・続、正編「事業と経営者」、続編「組織と人間」自由国民社、昭和31；野田一夫監修、現代経営研究会訳「現代の経営」上・下、エグゼクティブ・ブックス、ダイヤモンド社、昭和40。）

⑦ *America's Next Twenty Years.* Harper & Row, 1957.（中島正信・清井宏昭訳「オートメーションと新しい社会」ダイヤモンド社、昭和31。）

⑧ *The Landmarks of Tomorrow.* Harper & Row, 1959.（現代経営研究会訳「変貌する産業社会」ダイヤモンド社、昭和35。）

⑨ *Gedanken für die Zukunft.* Econ, 1959.（清水敏允訳「明日のための思想」ダイヤモンド社、昭和35。）

⑩ *Managing for Results.* Harper & Row, 1964.（野田一夫・村上恒夫訳「創造する経営者」ダイヤモンド社、昭和39。）

⑪ *The Effective Executive.* Harper & Row, 1967.（野田一夫・川村欣也訳「経営者の条件」ダイヤモンド社、昭和41。）

⑫ *The Age of Discontinuity: Guidelines to Our Changing Society.* Harper & Row, 1969.（林雄二郎訳「断絶の時代——来たるべき知識社会の構想」ダイヤモンド社、昭和44。）

⑬ *Preparing Tomorrow's Business Leaders Today.* Edited by Peter F.Drucker, Prentice-Hall, 1969.（中原伸之・篠原遵夫・武井清訳「今日なにをなすべきか

5

Although Drucker wrote primarily about management, he drew on a remarkably wide range of subjects—from literature and history, to sociology and theology, to Japanese art and culture. Seen here is a partial list of Drucker's books in both English and Japanese. Also shown is a letter to a friend in which Drucker discusses the novels he has been devouring. Charles Dickens and Jane Austen were particular favorites. "And I never read management books," Drucker asserted. "All they do is corrupt the style."

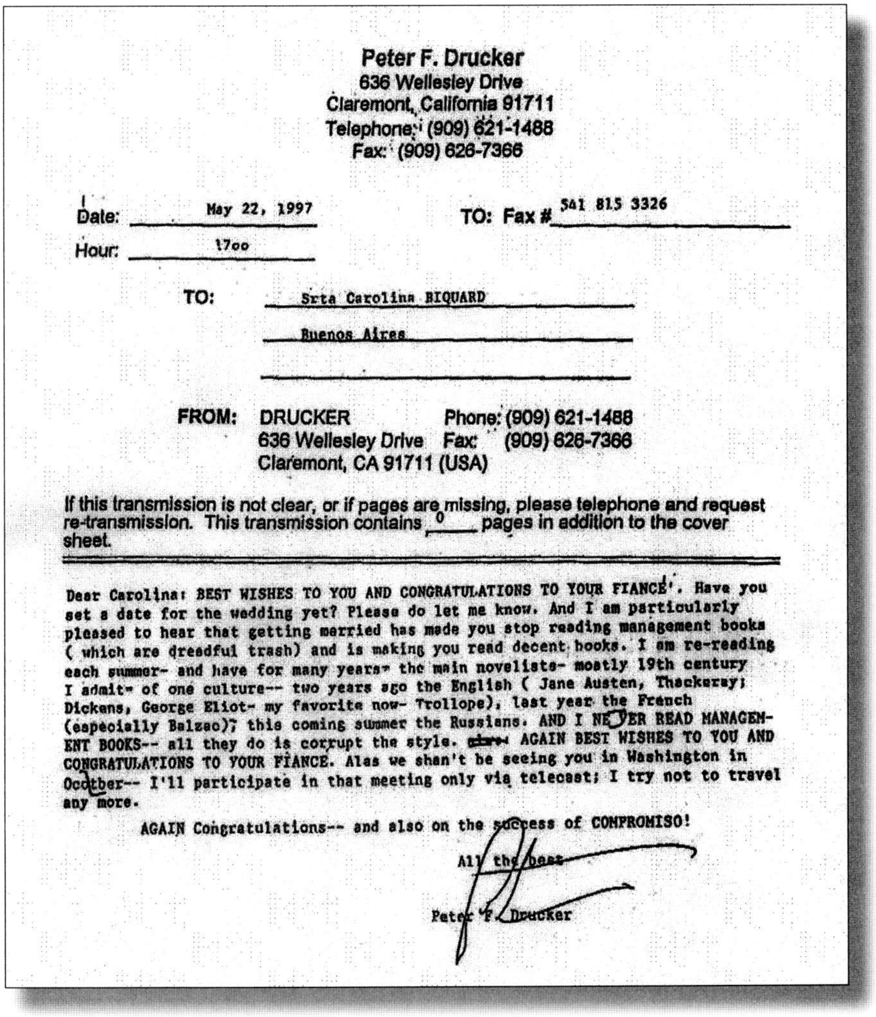

Peter F. Drucker
636 Wellesley Drive
Claremont, California 91711
Telephone: (909) 621-1488
Fax: (909) 626-7366

Date: _____ May 22, 1997 _____   TO: Fax # 541 815 3326 _____

Hour: _____ 1700 _____

TO: _____ Srta Carolina BIQUARD _____

_____ Buenos Aires _____

FROM: DRUCKER   Phone: (909) 621-1488
       636 Wellesley Drive   Fax: (909) 626-7366
       Claremont, CA 91711 (USA)

If this transmission is not clear, or if pages are missing, please telephone and request re-transmission. This transmission contains __0__ pages in addition to the cover sheet.

Dear Carolina: BEST WISHES TO YOU AND CONGRATULATIONS TO YOUR FIANCE'. Have you set a date for the wedding yet? Please do let me know. And I am particularly pleased to hear that getting married has made you stop reading management books (which are dreadful trash) and is making you read decent books. I am re-reading each summer- and have for many years- the main novelists- mostly 19th century I admit- of one culture-- two years ago the English (Jane Austen, Thackeray; Dickens, George Eliot- my favorite now- Trollope), last year the French (especially Balzac); this coming summer the Russians. AND I NEVER READ MANAGEM-ENT BOOKS-- all they do is corrupt the style. AGAIN BEST WISHES TO YOU AND CONGRATULATIONS TO YOUR FIANCE. Alas we shan't be seeing you in Washington in October-- I'll participate in that meeting only via telecast; I try not to travel any more.

   AGAIN Congratulations-- and also on the success of CONPROMISO!

              All the best

        Peter F. Drucker

If you asked Drucker what he did for a living, he wouldn't say "professor" or "consultant," although he was both of those things. Sometimes, if he wanted to be provocative, he'd say that he was a "social ecologist," observing our man-made environment the way a natural ecologist examines the biological world. Most of the time, though, he'd keep it simple: "I'm a writer." Shown here are some of the more workaday objects from Drucker's home office where he did his writing: his letter opener and his pencil holder.

Drucker had quite a bit to say about the advent of computers, and in the mid-1980s he hailed the word processor as "a genuine innovation that is radically changing office work." But Drucker himself never really got comfortable with a PC. Instead, he used a manual typewriter until he could no longer find parts for it. Then he switched to an electric—a Brother GX-6750. Shown here is the typewriter that Drucker wrote on until he died in 2005 at the age of 95. He tapped out the last 10 of his 39 books on this machine.

GX-6750
M REL
L MAR
R MAR
T SET
T CLR
AUTO
UNDLN
BOLD
RELOC
BS ½
W OUT
BACKSPACE
REV
INDEX
RETURN
EXPR
SHIFT
VIEW
CORRECT

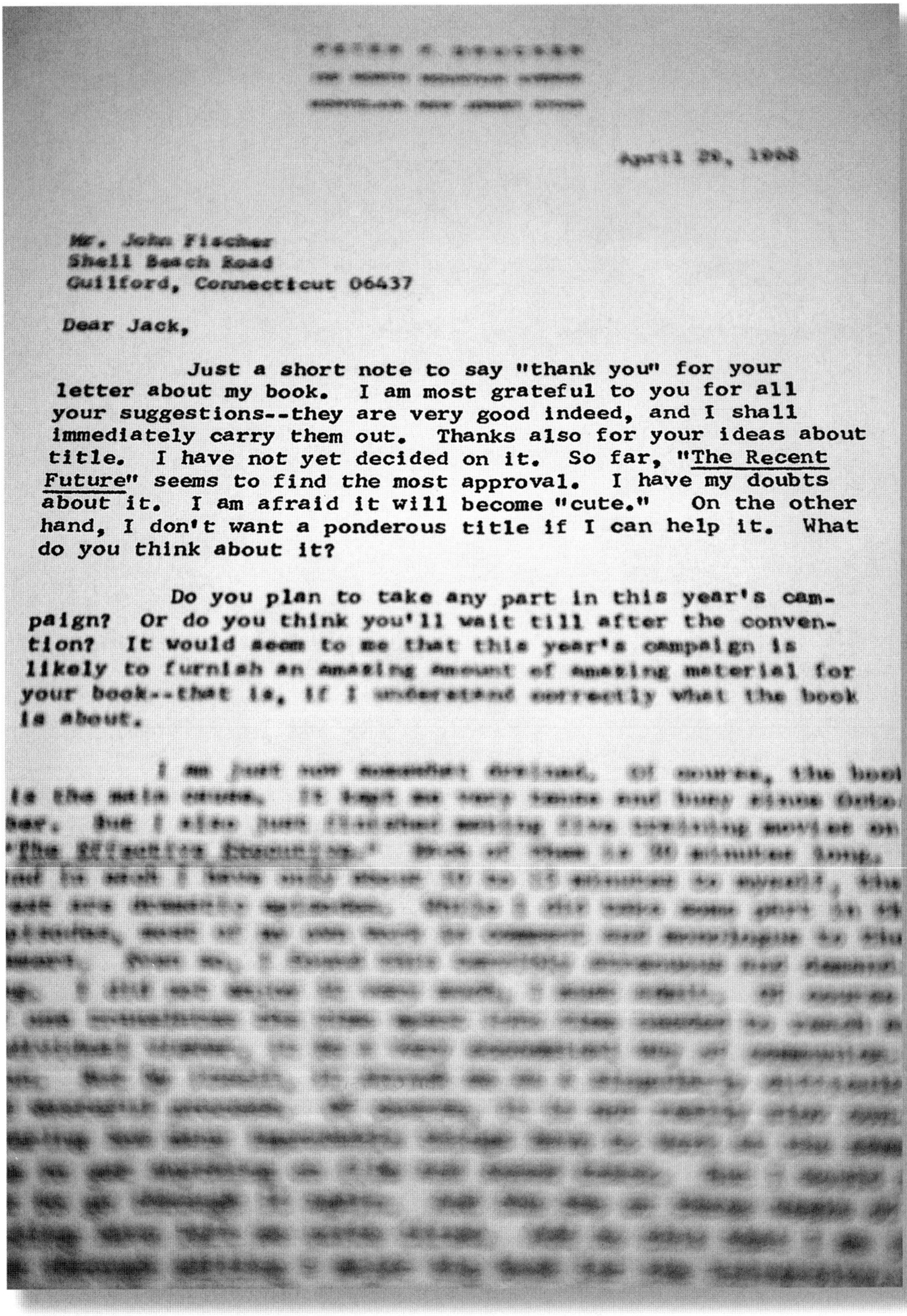

April 29, 1968

Mr. John Fischer
Shell Beach Road
Guilford, Connecticut 06437

Dear Jack,

Just a short note to say "thank you" for your letter about my book. I am most grateful to you for all your suggestions--they are very good indeed, and I shall immediately carry them out. Thanks also for your ideas about title. I have not yet decided on it. So far, "<u>The Recent Future</u>" seems to find the most approval. I have my doubts about it. I am afraid it will become "cute." On the other hand, I don't want a ponderous title if I can help it. What do you think about it?

Do you plan to take any part in this year's campaign? Or do you think you'll wait till after the convention? It would seem to me that this year's campaign is likely to furnish an amazing amount of amazing material for your book--that is, if I understand correctly what the book is about.

In the late 1960s, Drucker foresaw an era that would be beset by change—"in technology and in economic policy, in industry structures and in economic theory, in the knowledge needed to govern and to manage." Yet Drucker wasn't sure what to call the book exploring these themes. In a letter to a friend pictured here, Drucker revealed that he was leaning toward the title *The Recent Future*. In the end, however, he settled on another name: *The Age of Discontinuity*. Also shown here is an overstuffed collection of book reviews that Drucker clipped and kept.

When working as a young journalist in Frankfurt, Drucker was taught by the newspaper's editor in chief one of the most important lessons he ever learned: to methodically review his past work and set concrete goals about where to improve and what to concentrate on. All that said, Drucker never had any desire to become an editor himself, as explained in the 1958 letter shown here.

Peter F Drucker
138 North Mountain Avenue
Montclair, New Jersey

August 23, 1958

Dr Melvin Kranzberg
Department of Humanities
and Social Studies
Case Institute of Technology
Cleveland 6, Ohio

Dear Dr Kranzberg:

I am greatly flattered by you invitation to serve as an advisory editor of the quarterly journal "Technology and Culture" But I am afraid I have to turn down the invitation tempting though it is. I simply am not the right man for the job—not even if it is a sinecure.

In the first place I am not an editor; I am a writer And like practically all writers I am no good as an editor I do not read somebody else's manuscript for what he is trying to say but for what I can steal. I am not really interested in helping him express what he is after is his own best way; I am interted in how I would write this piece if it were mine. I have long ago decided that I have no business editing—just as I have long ago decided that I have no business reviewing.

Secondly, I have absolutely no competence. You and Lynn White confuse, I am afraid, interest in the subject with competence in it. Even as regards interest, I am certainly interested not in modern technology but in the six centuries between St. Benedict and St. Bonaventura, that is the centuries of the "first industrial revolution" But I am strictly a consumer and not a producer in this area.

And furthermore I have made it a rule (which I try not to break) not to accept any job on any board or committee unless I am willing and able to do a real job and to work hard. I know that I am not in a position to do this for your magazine; and rather than commit myself to a promise which I may not be able to keep, I'll stay out altogether

But I do appreciate you invitation and, needless to say, I should be very happy indeed to be useful as a reader and commentator whenever you feel I can make a contribution.

With best regards,

Sincerely,

PFD:mlc

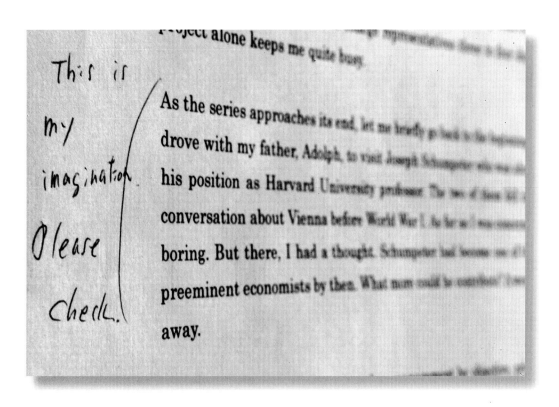

Still, like all good writers, Drucker was a sharp self-editor,
making sure to check the facts, as reflected in the margins of the
manuscript pictured here.

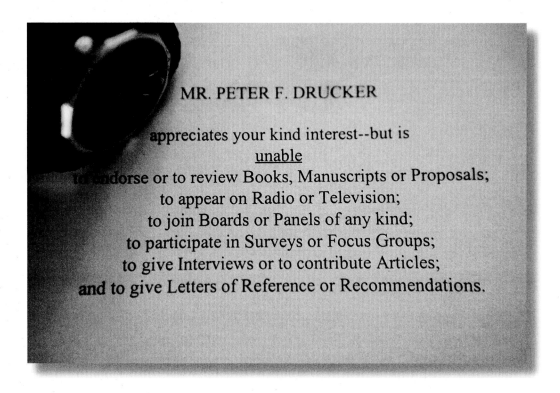

MR. PETER F. DRUCKER

appreciates your kind interest--but is
<u>unable</u>
to endorse or to review Books, Manuscripts or Proposals;
to appear on Radio or Television;
to join Boards or Panels of any kind;
to participate in Surveys or Focus Groups;
to give Interviews or to contribute Articles;
and to give Letters of Reference or Recommendations.

Drucker believed that in order to be effective, you have to be relentlessly focused. "We rightly consider keeping many balls in the air a circus stunt," he declared. As a writer, Drucker maintained his own incredible focus, a discipline that helped him to be extraordinarily prolific. Seen here are Drucker's wristwatch and a standard reply card that he used to turn down any and all manner of potential distractions, along with an example of the one thing that always commanded his attention: a working manuscript.

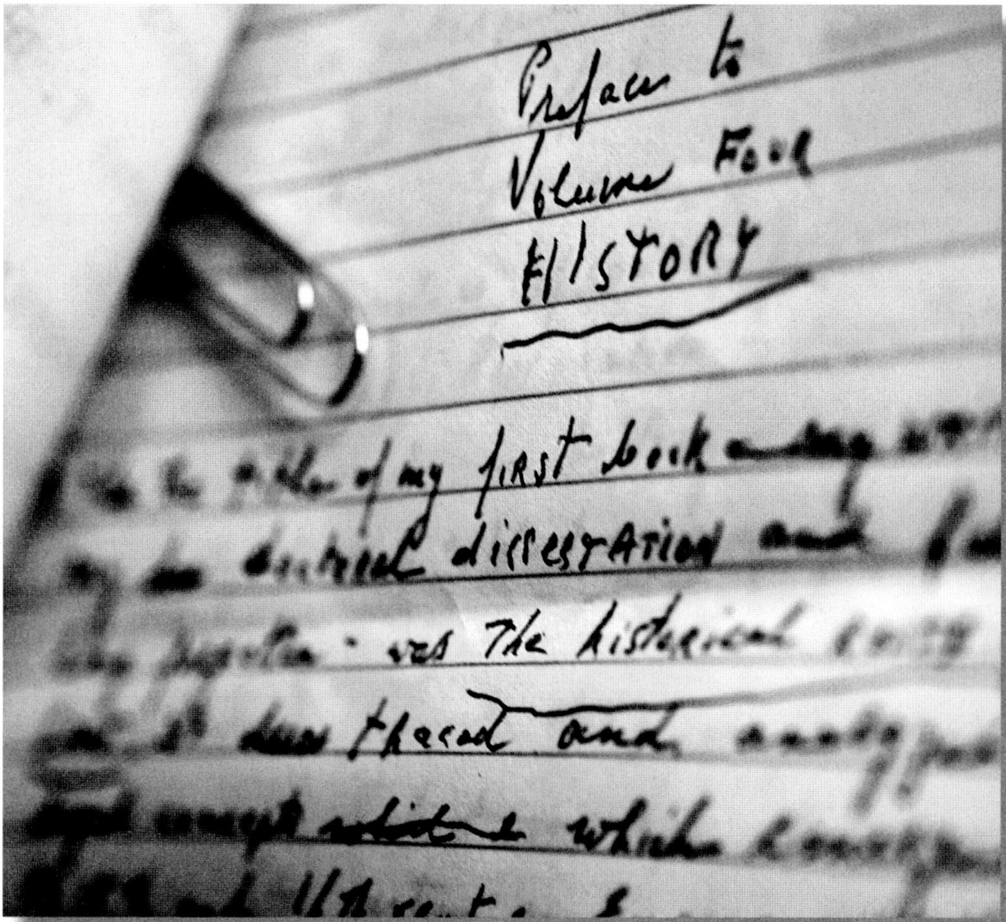
Preface to
Volume Four
HISTORY

Peter Drucker in the classroom

The Teacher

Interviewer: And what's your opinion of universities today?

Peter Drucker: Unprintable.

Interviewer: Why is that?

PD: The American university has been very badly damaged for having it so good these last 50 years.

Interviewer: In what way?

PD: It has become arrogant. It has become lazy. It has become self-righteous. And, above all, it believes that the student exists for the sake of the university.

But, look, I have taught since . . . I gave my first lecture . . . when I was in law school. I've made my living with my mouth wide open ever since. But I'm not an academician, in case you have any doubt. Teaching has never been my occupation; it's always been my avocation. I love to teach. But I never looked upon it as my occupation. It's my self-indulgence.

SARAH LAWRENCE COLLEGE
BRONXVILLE, NEW YORK

OFFICE OF THE PRESIDENT

TELEPHONE
BRONXVILLE 0700

June 24, 1940

Dr. Hardy Dillard
Institute of Public Affairs
University of Virginia
Charlottesville, Virginia

My dear Dr. Dillard:

Mr. Peter Drucker, who lives in Bronxville, has been to see me about the possibility of teaching here next year. It happens that we need someone to give a course in elementary economics taught in a much more realistic way than is usual in beginning courses in economics. By that I mean that we start in with problems that are important to the student, developing theory from those problems and putting her in touch with real situations through field work, etc. This does not mean less sound and scholarly work than one generally does with beginners but simply a course which treats economics as a part of every-day living rather than as a science set apart from politics, sociology and history. We would like to have this instructor carry on work in statistics with a few students also.

We found Mr. Drucker very stimulating indeed and think his point of view would be an excellent one to have on the faculty. I have no means of finding out anything about his teaching ability. He has suggested that I write to you and I am wondering if you have any light to throw on the subject. Do you think he could make his material simple enough for intelligent beginners? Perhaps if you would tell me something about him as a person that might help us to form an idea of how well he would work with our students. We do very little lecturing at the College but conduct our classes by the discussion and conference method which, of course, entails having a person who not only has insight into the needs of individual students but is a good listener as well as a good talker and is provocative in discussion.

I would be very grateful for any information you may be able to give me about Mr. Drucker.

Very sincerely yours,

Constance Warren
President

CW/M

(Typed after Miss Warren had left the office)

Drucker counted his fourth-grade teachers from Austria, Miss
Elsa and Miss Sophy, as two of the most significant figures in
his life. They "taught me that teaching and learning, of high
quality and with a high level of intensity and enjoyment, are
possible," he wrote. Pictured here are two items bookending
Drucker's own teaching career: a 1940 letter inquiring as to his
abilities in the classroom and an award from Claremont Graduate
University alumni (with the Drucker School of Management in
the background).

"Teachers start out with passion," Drucker wrote. "Pedagogues acquire it as they become intoxicated with the enlightenment of the student. For the smile of learning on the student's face is more addictive than any drug." Drucker's own passion took him from Sarah Lawrence to Bennington College to New York University to Claremont Graduate University. Seen here is a plaque given to Drucker for his many contributions to CGU, as well as one of the many letters that Drucker received from his students for having a profound impact on their lives.

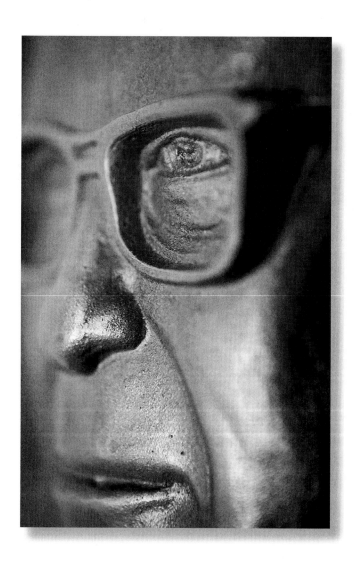

May 15, 1998

Professor Peter Drucker
636 Wellesley
Claremont, California 74171

Dear Peter,

I wanted to write and thank you again for the many things that you and your classes have taught me in the last 12 years. You have changed my life and work and my direction in a very positive way.

In 1985 I came to your class as a very burned out community college administrator and left extremely inspired to move in a more positive direction. Armed with a better plan, new skills and new strategies, I launched into the building of a new student center building on our campus testing many of your methods along the way.... this is something I would have never tried before taking your classes, watching you teach, watching your consulting and reading your books.

Based upon one of your classes and a conversation we had during and after one of your classes, I decided to change from trying to become a community college president to a management teacher, part-time consultant and a little bit of writing. This move made me a whole lot happier and much more productive. To date in the last 10 years, I have taught about 2800 + students about Business and Management about 40 percent almost straight from your classes, seminars and alumni days. When they leave class they know a lot of ████ ████ Management. They are managers in most Las Vegas Casinos, Utilities

Drucker didn't always look favorably on higher education. "When a subject becomes totally obsolete," he said, "we make it a required course." And those in higher education didn't always appreciate Drucker, who wrote for practitioners, not for members of the academy. "They hated his guts," Tom Peters once remarked. Nonetheless, Drucker received honorary doctorates from universities in the United States, Belgium, Czechoslovakia, Great Britain, Japan, Spain, and Switzerland. Shown here is a close-up of one of Drucker's doctoral hoods.

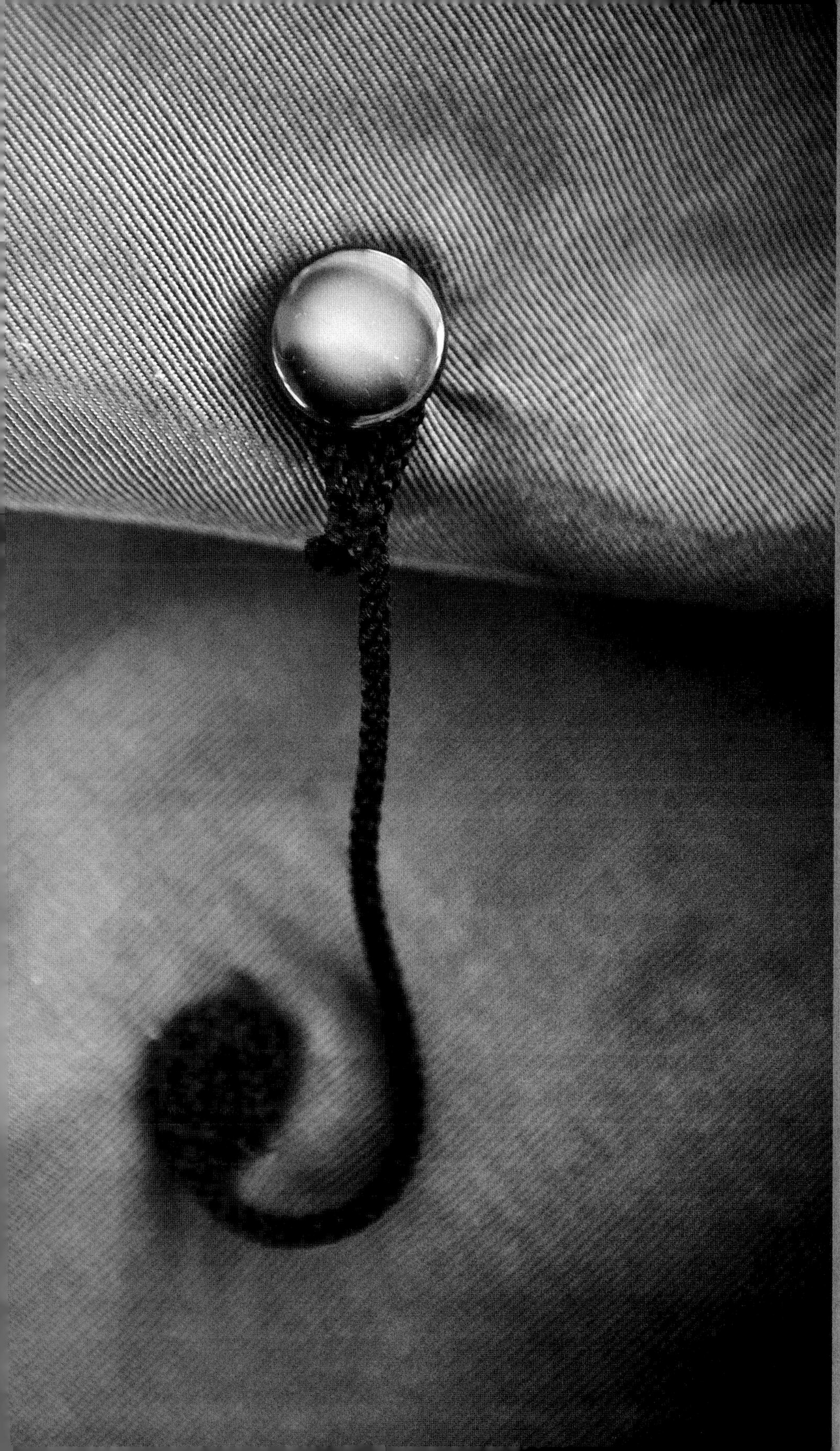

NEW YORK UNIVERSITY

WASHINGTON SQUARE, NEW YORK, N. Y. 10003

Office of the President

December 9, 1968

Dear Professor Drucker:

The publication today of the volume entitled <u>Preparing Tomorrow's Business Leaders Today</u> reminds us of the happy occasion last May at which many of the original papers reprinted in that volume were first presented at a symposium celebrating the fiftieth anniversary of the Graduate School of Business Administration of New York University.

You have had the lion's share of responsibility for this magnificent symposium. You personally obtained the cooperation of outstanding leaders from education, government, and industry. You organized their contributions, wrote a number of the most important chapters, and edited the entire volume. This is indeed a notable addition to your many outstanding works on political and economic subjects.

Now that you are entering the sixtieth year of your life, it is fitting that we should recall some of the highlights of your distinguished career. After the Gymnasium in Vienna, you took your doctorate in public and international law at the University of Frankfurt, and you served as an economist for an international banking house in London. You came to the United States in 1937, continued as a banking advisor, and became the American correspondent for a group of British newspapers. You have always been an astute observer of the American business scene. You taught Politics and Philosophy at Bennington College from 1942 to 1949, and in 1950 you came to New York University as a professor of Management.

You have proved to be an effective teacher who has the ability to develop in students the capacity to think clearly about the process of management and to help them utilize this knowledge in their roles as managers of large organizations. And throughout your academic life, you have continued as an advisor to major business enterprises. Your writings have earned you an international reputation for insight and creative thinking in the fields of management, business policy, and organization. Probably more than any other academician, you have succeeded in bridging the gap between the practical man of business and the theoretician.

To the many honorary degrees, medals, and other awards you have received in recognition of your exceptional achievements, I now add the Presidential Citation of New York University.

Sincerely yours,

James M. Hester

Professor Peter F. Drucker
New York University

Drucker's first taste of teaching came in Austria when he helped a classmate who was struggling in Latin, Greek, and math. "Suddenly I enjoyed all of these subjects. . . . And I learned them because I had to explain them. And suddenly it hit me: The best way to learn is to teach." Seen here is a letter telling Drucker that he will receive NYU's highest honor, along with a gift from one of Drucker's CGU students. "This book and your book *On the Profession of Management* have been the most motivating works I have ever read," the inscription inside says.

St. James Street
London SW1A 1H9
England

Dear Bill Emmott:

I greatly appreciate the story on me in the October 1 issue of <u>The Economist</u>. Please convey to the writer my warmest thanks.

In fact, you cannot possibly imagine how much the story means to me. It is <u>l'accolade supréme</u> as <u>The Economist</u> has been mentor and authority for me all my adult life. But for this reason also I ask your indulgence in my pointing out one <u>factual</u> misstatement in the story. You write "he has spent <u>most</u> of his career as a luminary in the relative obscurity of Claremont College, California." Actually, the bulk of my management books – six out of nine – were written before I went to Claremont, and mostly during the 21 years – 1950 to 1971 – when I taught full-time as Professor of Management at the Graduate Business School of New York University. For ten of these years, I also taught part-time as a Visiting Professor at the Wharton School of the University of Pennsylvania. These two were then the largest graduate business schools in the US, hardly obscure places and anything but placid or non-competitive. And during the years in New York, that is, between 1950 and 1971, I also did the bulk of my <u>business</u> consulting. Since then the center of my consulting work have been non-profits, especially churches.

As to "Harvard or Stanford," both have courted me, and more than once. In the end I always said "No." I could not accept their ethics, or lack thereof. Both schools openly boast of their training students to become rich. That to me is not

[...]

join the Harva... ...ulty. In the end the Committee despite these objections accepted eve..., ...ngle place I submitted because of its quality and scholarship.

As to my living in the "obscurity" of Claremont, I came here in 1971, already 62 years old, because I was about to reach the compulsory retirement age (then 65) at New York University and would have had to stop teaching – and I only learn when I teach. Claremont offered to let me teach as long as I wanted. No one – least of all I – then expected that I'd last more than ten years. But I still teach full time, at age 85

Claremont also offered a fellow about to be condemned to idleness a new beginning as an educational innovator and entrepreneur· to start and build a management school based on <u>my</u> principles:

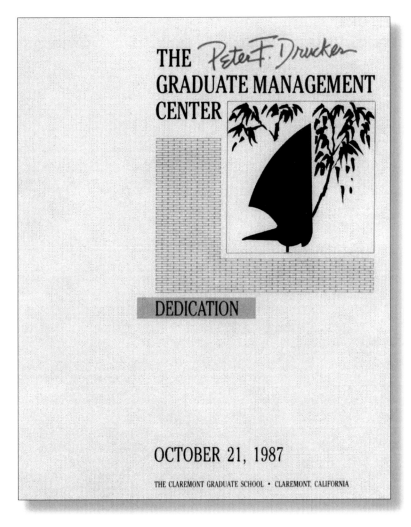

THE *Peter F. Drucker*
GRADUATE MANAGEMENT
CENTER

DEDICATION

OCTOBER 21, 1987

THE CLAREMONT GRADUATE SCHOOL • CLAREMONT, CALIFORNIA

Shown here is a letter from Drucker to the *Economist* explaining the appeal of teaching in Claremont, along with a program from the 1987 dedication of the Peter F. Drucker Graduate Management Center. A decade later, the center was rechristened the Peter F. Drucker Graduate School of Management. Yet Drucker wasn't typical of those who get their name on a campus building. That same year, he decried the soaring cost of college tuition in the United States "without any visible improvement in either the content or the quality of education."

Drucker's lectures were famous for the way he would meander from one topic to the next before magically tying everything together by the end of the class. All the while, his students would sit spellbound, hanging on his every word, as Drucker's warmth and charm transformed "the chilly lecture hall to the size and comfort of a living room," as one former student characterized it. Shown here is a syllabus from "The Management Process," a course that Drucker offered at CGU in the mid-1970s.

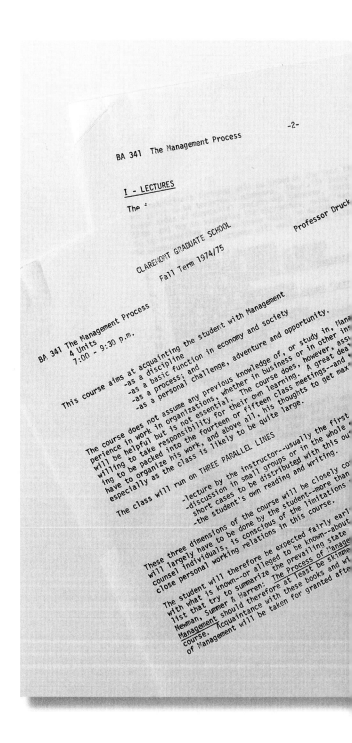

BA 341 The Management Process   -2-

I - LECTURES

The

CLAREMONT GRADUATE SCHOOL   Professor Druck

Fall Term 1974/75

BA 341 The Management Process
4 Units
7:00 - 9:30 p.m.

This course aims at acquainting the student with Management
        -as a discipline
        -as a basic function in economy and society
        -as a process; and
        -as a personal challenge, adventure and opportunity.

The course does not assume any previous knowledge of, or study in, Mana
perience in work in organizations, whether in business or in other ins
will be helpful but is not essential. The course does, however, assu
willing to take responsibility for their own learning. A great dea
ing to be packed into the fourteen or fifteen class meetings--and
have to organize his work, and above all, his thoughts to get max
especially as the class is likely to be quite large.

The class will run on THREE PARALLEL LINES
        -lecture by the instructor--usually the first
        -discussion in small groups or in the whole
        short cases to be distributed with this ou
        -the student's own reading and writing.

These three dimensions of the course will be closely co
will largely have to be done by the student--more than
counsel individuals, is conscious of the limitations
close personal working relations in this course.

The student will therefore be expected fairly earl
with what is known--or alleged to be known--about
1st that try to summarize: The Process of Manage
Newman, Summer & Warren should therefore at least be skimme
Management. Acquaintance with these books and wi
course. of Management will be taken for granted afte

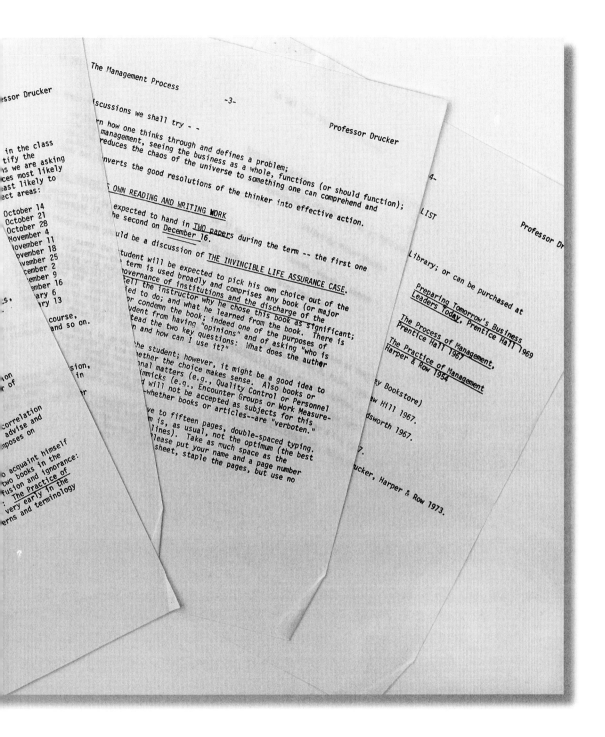

The Management Process
-3-
Professor Drucker

iscussions we shall try --

rn how one thinks through and defines a problem;
management, seeing the business as a whole, functions (or should function);
reduces the chaos of the universe to something one can comprehend and

nverts the good resolutions of the thinker into effective action.

in the class
tify the
s we are asking
ces most likely
ast likely to
ect areas:

October 14
October 21
October 28
November 4
November 11
ovember 18
vember 25
cember 2
ember 9
ember 16
ary 6
ary 13

course,
and so on.

OWN READING AND WRITING WORK

expected to hand in TWO papers during the term -- the first one
he second on December 16.

uld be a discussion of THE INVINCIBLE LIFE ASSURANCE CASE.

tudent will be expected to pick his own choice out of the
term is used broadly and comprises any book (or major
overnance of institutions and the discharge of the
ell the instructor why he chose this book as significant;
ed to do; and what he learned from the book. There is
or condemn the book; indeed one of the purposes of
dent from having "opinions" and of asking "who is
stead the two key questions: What does the author
n and how can I use it?"

he student; however, it might be a good idea to
hether the choice makes sense. Also books or
nal matters (e.g., Quality Control or Personnel
mmicks (e.g., Encounter Groups or Work Measure-
d will not be accepted as subjects for this
--whether books or articles--are "verboten."

ve to fifteen pages, double-spaced typing.
m is, as usual, not the optimum (the best
lines). Take as much space as the
lease put your name and a page number
sheet, staple the pages, but use no

correlation
advise and
mposes on

acquaint himself
wo books in the
fusion and ignorance:
: The Practice of
very early in the
erns and terminology

4-

LIST

Professor Dr

Library; or can be purchased at

Preparing Tomorrow's Business
Leaders Today, Prentice Hall 1969

The Process of Management,
Prentice Hall 1967

The Practice of Management
Harper & Row 1954

ey Bookstore)

aw Hill 1967.

dsworth 1967.

rucker, Harper & Row 1973.

Peter Drucker with Intel Corp.'s Andy Grove

The
Business
Consultant

Interviewer: You think managers are adolescents? In what sense?

Peter Drucker: They yield to peer pressure. If a fellow CEO on the golf course says, "We are using this, and we wouldn't do without it," you have to do it, too. The last 20 years have been very unsettling. Executives really don't understand the world in which they live. But bandwagon psychology is nothing new. When I was growing up in Vienna, everybody felt the need to be psychoanalyzed. And there was a time when every child older than four years had to have his tonsils out. So this is not confined to management.

Interviewer: One of the reasons I admire your work so much is you've never really been an evangelist for any single thing.

PD: No. I was taught at an early age that you make the diagnosis before you operate. And nine times out of ten, when you make the diagnosis, you don't operate. You just wait. You're going to have to put that foot in a cast and for six months try not to step on it. But American management has been no more fad-conscious than any other. Japanese and European managers have been just as oriented to fads.

GENERAL ELECTRIC COMPANY

LAMP DIVISION

ADMINISTRATION DEPARTMENT

NELA PARK   CLEVELAND 12   OHIO   •   TELEPHONE GLENVILLE 1-6600

May 20, 1954

Mr. Peter F. Drucker,
138 N. Mountain Avenue,
Montclair, N. J.

Dear Peter:

All of us who comprised the "Task Force" on the subject of Lamp Division Objectives and Structure, want to express to you our deep appreciation for the tremendous help you rendered during the course of the survey.

Your objectivity and uncanny knack of focusing our attention on the main target were most sorely needed on several occasions, as I am sure you know. In addition, you gave us a much needed "lift" at those times when we really needed it. In short, each of us takes this most inadequate means of saying, many, many thanks.

Sincerely,

F. J. Borch

F. J. BORCH

FJB/GW
c:DIMillham

On behalf of the eight of us.

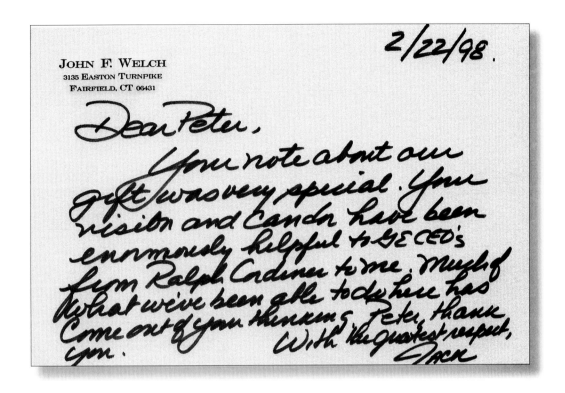

JOHN F. WELCH
3135 EASTON TURNPIKE
FAIRFIELD, CT 06431

2/22/98.

Dear Peter,

Your note about our gift was very special. Your vision and candor have been enormously helpful to GE CEO's from Ralph Cordiner to me. Much of what we've been able to do here has come out of your thinking, Peter, thank you.

With the greatest respect,

Jack

"If you weren't already in the business," Drucker asked, "would you enter it today? And if the answer is no, what are you going to do about it?" These questions, asked of General Electric CEO Jack Welch, led Welch to his pivotal strategy of fixing, selling, or closing every business in which GE was not number one or number two in the market. Drucker had a long history of advising GE's top brass, starting in the 1950s with CEO Ralph Cordiner. Pictured here are two letters to Drucker: one from Fred Borch, who would become CEO in 1967, and the other from Welch.

Another big fan of Drucker's was Donald Keough, the president of Coca-Cola, who appreciated his counselor's constant call to action. "Drucker purified my mind," Keough said. "He would tell me after each session, 'Don't tell me you had a wonderful meeting with me. Tell me what you're going to do on Monday that's different.'" Shown here is a 1992 consulting report on global branding and marketing challenges that Drucker wrote for the soft drink giant, along with a pair of Drucker's reading glasses.

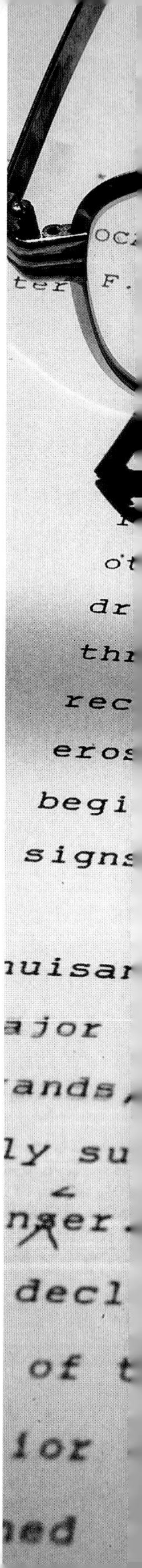

2)   BRAND CHALLENGES

Coca Cola is the world's best known brand.   The
most important asset the company
And The Coca-Cola Company has been singularly
ssful in establishing additional brands as lead
market, whether brands of other Cola drinks,
carbonated drinks, or non-carbonated fruit

That the changes in distribution channels
n serious erosion of brand equity and brand
tion is therefore surely a major concern.
has already gone quite far in the U.S.   It
g in Europe.   And I understand that the fi
such erosion are visible in Japan.
ty years ago house brands were an occasi
rather than a threat.   In the U.S. only
ilers had successfully established hous
rs Roebuck and R. H. Macy.   In the U.
sful house brands were those of Marks
he A&P in the 1950s and 1960s tried
by pushing its own brands.   But eve
A & P brands, e.g. its coffee, were
lity and attractively priced, they
& P's downfall

June 17, 1974

Mr. Richard H. Jenrette
Donaldson, Lufkin & Jenrette, Inc.
140 Broadway
New York, New York   10005

Dear Dick:

You asked me to reflect on my day and a half with you and your
associates last week and to write you should anything occur to
me that we did not discuss. I have been going over my notes
pretty carefully and I think we covered everything that was on
your agenda. But it might serve a useful purpose if I try to
summarize my main conclusions again.

1.   It seems to me absolutely essential that you face up
to the need to make a decision regarding your position, direction
and scope in the securities business. Your problem is that you
have attained your original objectives. The basic premises on
which you, Bill Donaldson and Dan Lufkin founded the firm ten
years ago have been brilliantly proven right - and as a result
you have reached your original objective. This, in many ways,
is the most dangerous situation one can be in. For there is
then always the temptation to believe that one can, or should,
keep on by doing more of what proved so successful in the past.
Actually, at this point, to do what has been so successful in
the past is always the wrong thing; and to do more of it is to
be doubly wrong. It is simply not adequate then to be able to
do a little better what by now almost everybody can do and everybody is trying to do. To do what by now has become common strategy
a little better than the rest cannot be any distinction. Yet it
becomes increasingly expensive. It is therefore, on principle,
the wrong strategy.

What is needed in such a situation is the courage to face up
to the tough question: "If we were not in this business today
would we go into it? And if we were to go into it, what would
be the right policy for tomorrow, the policy that would give us
a distinction, if not true uniqueness?"

I am not qualified to have an opinion on what the answer to this
question should or might be. My own inclination would be to say

"A success that has outlived its usefulness may, in the end, be more damaging than failure," Drucker wrote. In the documents shown here—a 1974 letter to the investment bank Donaldson, Lufkin & Jenrette and a 2001 memo to Procter & Gamble—Drucker underlined this very point. "Your problem is that you have attained your original objectives," Drucker told DLJ. "This, in many ways, is the most dangerous situation one can be in." Similarly, Drucker warned P&G: "It may be precisely the very perfection of the P&G system that has become a straightjacket."

Comments on P&G Position Paper
by Peter Drucker

Overview:
Your position paper persuasively argues that P&G has traditionally focused on optimizing its Market Capital, i.e., its Brands. What is thoughtfully proposed is to supplement the optimization of your market capital with optimizing your Intellection Capital, i.e., the information, knowledge and passion of your performing people.

Introduction
P&G has not performed well in recent years, and malperformance began well before the slowdown in the U.S. economy. In a consumer boom you actually lost market share in some of your most important brands. There are three plausible explanations for such a development:

1) Incompetent people
2) The basic assumptions and strategies on which the business operates no longer fit reality – the market, the environment, the demographics, or distribution system,
3) The knowledge, competence, and drive of performing people are misdirected or inadequately utilized.

Explanation #1 can be dismissed out-of-hand. The same people who today do not produce results, performed magnificently only yesterday. There is no reason to believe that large numbers of people who have shown a long period of high performance, would suddenly stop performing.

Explanation #2 is certainly of high relevance – but it is also being attacked, and vigorously. P&G is re-thinking its basic Theory of the Business, adapting it, changing it, re-focusing it. In fact, P&G has already taken more than one big step towards a strategy based on the Changing Demographics. The acquisition of Clairol, for instance, was brilliant, though not yet comprehended by Wall Street. Clairol demographics take off where the Pampers demographics leave off.

Your position paper is concerned primarily with Explanation #3. Its policy conclusions supplement the policy conclusions on the Theory of the Business. Indeed, unless the Theory of the Business and the strategies to make it operational are correct, no policy in respect to People and Intellectual Capital will produce results. But conversely, the most brilliant strategies will be ineffectual unless buttressed by the right policies and strategies in respect to People. People rather than Strategies produce results.

Coming back to the Overview, your paper argues that, traditionally P&G has focused on optimizing its Market Capital – Brands, and has treated the information, knowledge and passion of people as an "input", i.e., the traditional economist's "labor", and a "cost". Your paper proposes to consider and to utilize the information, knowledge and passion of performing people as "Intellectual Capital" – that is – as the central resource for the entire company rather than as an input into a specialty, department, product or market segment, and as something to produce a substantial "Rent" that is a return highly dis-proportionate to its costs and therefore, a major Producer of Wealth.

The Business Consultant

67

the early 1980s, Drucker prodded Edward Jones to rethink its growth strategy. Rather than just expanding into rural and small-town markets, Drucker advised, the brokerage firm's priority should be to give its customers terrific service and no-frills investments, regardless of their location. Huge success followed. Seen here is Drucker's plaque from the Edward Jones corporate Hall of Fame, along with a letter that Drucker wrote to Sears when he signed the company on as a client. In it, he made clear how he'd be compensated: send the money only if it's been worth it.

Peter Drucker

An authority on management, Peter advised Edward Jones for over two decades. He encouraged us to define our clients by mindset, not by geography, which led to the firm's metropolitan expansion. Peter often referred to himself as an intermittent member of Edward Jones' senior management.

March 29, 1955

Mr. James C. Worthy
Assistant to the Chairman
Sears Roebuck & Company
Chicago 7, Illinois

Dear Jim:

I want to tell you how very happy I am to have an opportunity to work with you again and how very proud I am to be asked to contribute to the work of Sears-Roebuck.

As I told you, I have learned to stick to a few simple policies in my relationship with a client. And I should like to spell them out again--just to make sure that they are clear.

In the first place, I do not want the client to be committed to any contractual relationship with me. Even where I work with a client on the basis of a retainer, the client is able to cancel it at any time and for any reason. And where there is no retainer arrangement--as in my understanding with you--the client can simply stop the relationship by not assigning me any more work.

Secondly, I prefer--very much prefer--to have definite and concrete work assigned rather than a general agreement to "work together". Now, precisely because most, if not all, of my work deals with top management problems of business policy, management organization or management methods, I think it best to avoid anything of the fuzzy and vague relationship.

Thirdly, I have long ago adopted the Sears slogan of "Satisfaction guaranteed or your money back", by which I mean that I will not bill a client unless he has been satisfied with my work. As I told you, a management consultant in my line of work simply cannot afford to have any one company around which feels that it has not gotten value for the money paid.

In 1989, Drucker asked the members of ServiceMaster's board, "What is your business?" Their reply: cleaning floors, killing weeds, and so on. "You are all wrong," Drucker said. "Your business is the training and development of people"—an insight that led to a dramatic shift in the way ServiceMaster motivated and cared for its employees. Seen here is an eighty-fifth birthday

greeting to Drucker from ServiceMaster's workers along with a
fan letter from a smaller company, highlighting the broad scope
of businesses with which Drucker worked.

**JAMES M. VARDAMAN
& CO., INC.**

FOREST MANAGEMENT
SPECIALISTS
P.O. DRAWER 22766
JACKSON, MISSISSIPPI 39225
601-354-3123

29 July 1987

Editor
The Wall Street Journal
200 Liberty St.
New York, NY 10281

Dear Sir:

Some consultants may find Peter Drucker's advice impractical and have
trouble translating it into actions, but we never did. During a total of seven days in 1973 and 1977, he spoke directly to our problems
and helped us through the period of extraordinary growth that sinks
many companies. He gave us, not techniques, but understanding. He
insisted that we learn what our business was and should be, build
upon the strengths of our staff members and make their weaknesses
irrelevant, and demand and reward nothing but superior performance.
Although none of us at that time had studied anything but <u>forest</u> management, we knew immediately how to apply what we learned from him.

He gave us something else that is rarely mentioned. Once he helps a
manager understand what the manager's role really is, Peter insists
that the manager's practices meet the very highest moral standards,
that he appeal only to the highest instincts of those he manages.
When you follow Peter's code, you don't need to worry about violating
many of the laws that scare many managers. And every now and then,
you see a tiny sign that you have made the world a better place to
work in.

Sincerely,

James M. Vardaman

The Business Consultant

Yamazaki Baking introduces 5,000 new products a year—
an outpouring of innovation that it credits, in large part, to
Drucker's guidance. "A key to innovation is to try not to be
brilliant, but to be simple," Yamazaki's CEO, Nobuhiro Iijima, has
said, echoing Drucker's philosophy. "If you try to produce

brilliant results, you tend to use big seeds. It is better to sow small seeds and make them bear big fruit." Pictured here is an award that Yamazaki gave to Drucker, along with a letter from a firm handling another kind of bread: Bank One.

Finance One Corporation   Tel 614 244 3070
825 Tech Center Drive
Columbus OH 43271 1083

February 10, 1999

Dr Peter Drucker
Professor
Claremont College
636 Wellesley Drive
Claremont, CA 91711

Dear Dr Drucker·

The insights you shared during our videotaped discussion in December were exceptionally helpful. In fact, they were so meaningful to our business that we decided to include a key portion of the video at the January 1999 Finance One National Sales Conference in Orlando, attended by 800 top sales and marketing performers.

Our conference participants were intrigued with your observation that financial institutions are social entities. Our managers, in particular, appreciated your fresh ideas on human resources, which will affect the way we think about and approach our people. In addition, your input has been very helpful to me in the development of the Breakthrough Leadership process. (Colin Powell, our guest speaker the night your video aired, also noted your insightful comments in his speech.)

As a result of the impact you made—both at our conference and toward the long-term success of Finance One—our executive team has selected you to receive the BANK ONE Visionary Award. The award is presented each year to a leader whose exceptional vision, commitment and courage to explore new ideas have inspired our people   You will receive the Visionary Award by separate cover in the next few days.

Dr Drucker, you and I have had several discussions over the years. You continue to be an inspiration to me—and to the international business community   I look forward to visiting with you again.

Warmest regards,

Don Winkler
Chairman and CEO

September 4, 2001

The President
The White House
Washington, D.C. 20036

Dear Mr. President:

I am writing to add my voice to those urging you to consider Peter F. Drucker for the presidential Medal of Freedom with Distinction.

As other business leaders such as Jack Welch and A. G. Lafley have emphasized in recent letters to you, Peter Drucker's groundbreaking concepts of management have contributed immeasurably to America's economic strength and business leadership. Just as important, his insights and ideas have had impact far beyond the boardroom and the factory floor. The Peter F. Drucker Foundation for NonProfit Management has been uniquely successful in bringing sound business principles to non-profit and charitable organizations. (The Foundation's current president, Frances Hesselbein, was also awarded the Presidential Medal of Freedom in 1998.)

While Peter's contributions to American business are well-known, he also played a major but lesser-known role in America's industrial mobilization and victory in World War II. Apart from advising leaders in Washington, D.C., he spent numerous hours in many plants observing and noting what it took to organize, train, re-group, and motivate the work force for conversion from production of consumer goods to war material. The General Motors plant in Wilmington, Delaware, which converted from building automobiles to fighter planes, is one example. As Peter noted in a recent interview, "The sergeants won the war on the battlefield and the first-line supervisors won it in the plants." Peter was, in a real sense, one of the generals responsible for training those "sergeants" in the plants.

Today, Peter Drucker's ideas continue to energize and unleash the creativity and productivity of men and women in all walks of life. He truly embodies the spirit of the Medal of Freedom and I urge you to consider him for this honor.

Sincerely,

Jack Smith

Drucker's first peek inside a major company came at the invitation of General Motors. The result was his 1946 landmark, *Concept of the Corporation*. GM hated Drucker's book for asserting that some of the company's policies were outdated. Still, all was evidently forgiven years later, judging by John Smith's letter, shown here. Drucker liked to refer to himself not as a consultant but as "an insultant" who "scolds clients for a fee." But it's hard to read David Rockefeller's tender words, also shown here, and believe that Drucker was always so tough.

30 ROCKEFELLER PLAZA
NEW YORK N Y 10112

ROOM 5600

(212) 649 5600
November 30, 1999

Dear Peter:

    I have read a number of articles about you lately
indicating that you are cutting back to some degree from your
very heavy schedule. The articles reminded me of the times we
used to see one another when I was still with The Chase.

    One of the pieces spoke of you appropriately as "the
father of modern management." From my perspective, that was a
fully justified accolade. Your approach to management always
appealed to me as being more philosophical than dogmatic.
Without having been as careful a student of your books as I might
have been, you gave me a sense of management style which I found
very helpful during my years as a banker.

    I have no other purpose in writing this letter other than
to tell you that I feel that in many ways I learned more about
how to be a manager from you than from anyone else I can think
of. I always enjoyed the all too rare conversations we had and
only regret that I did not take greater advantage than I did of
your wisdom as a teacher.

    I hope things are going well for you. If you have time
some day when you pass through New York, I hope you will give me
a call. It would be fun to exchange some reflections.

    With best regards,

Sincerely,

David

David Rockefeller

Dr. Peter F. Drucker
636 Wellesley Drive
Claremont, California 91711

Peter Drucker in the 1960s, when the White House sought his wisdom

The
Government
Counsel

Interviewer: How did you first begin consulting for the government?

Peter Drucker: Like everything else, I never looked for anything. It always came to me. And this was, you've heard of such a thing as World War II? Well, they came to me and wanted me, period.

Interviewer: Who was it that came to you?

PD: Something called the Board of Economic Warfare. . . . They wanted to hire me full time and after a few weeks they decided and I decided that I didn't want it. I was to be the number two man in it or the number three man, I don't know. And I hated it. And I know that I'm no good at all in a big organization. I don't belong in it. I am a loner. And so after a very short time, maybe after a couple of weeks, we decided that I didn't belong. They decided that I didn't belong. And I remained a consultant.

Drucker studiously avoided any kind of partisan affiliation, as evinced by his 1959 letter regarding his possibly assisting the Republican Party, shown here. At the same time, he was proud to serve any president when asked, as illustrated by the short note from President Johnson, also shown here. All the while, Drucker looked to those occupying the Oval Office for lessons on leadership. Not long before he died, Drucker picked out a Democrat (Harry Truman) and a Republican (Ronald Reagan) as the two most effective presidents of the previous 100 years.

PETER F. DRUCKER

138 NORTH MOUNTAIN AVENUE

MONTCLAIR, NEW JERSEY

July 31, 1959

Professor Robert E. Rathbarn
University of Colorado
Boulder, Colorado

Dear Professor Rathburn,

I am afraid I was under a misapprehension when I talked to you on the telephone the other day. I thought that your Committee had been appointed by the President of the United States and was charged with basic, long-range thinking for the United States Government. I found out a few minutes later, when talking to Mr. Percy, that this is not correct, and that your Committee is appointed by, and works for, the Republican Party.

I have always, as a matter of principle, been available to the Government of the United States. But I have long since decided, also as a matter of principle, that my only connection with a political party- if any- would be as a candidate (and that's most unlikely to happen, I'd say). I am therefore forced to decline your kind invitation to read the reports and to comment on them- I have read them though, found them stimulating but also found myself with the question in my mind whether good intentions on every political question really add up to a political program and to a policy.

I return the documents you so kindly sent me. With best regards

Sincerely yours,

copies to Mr. Charles Percy
Mr. James C. Worthy

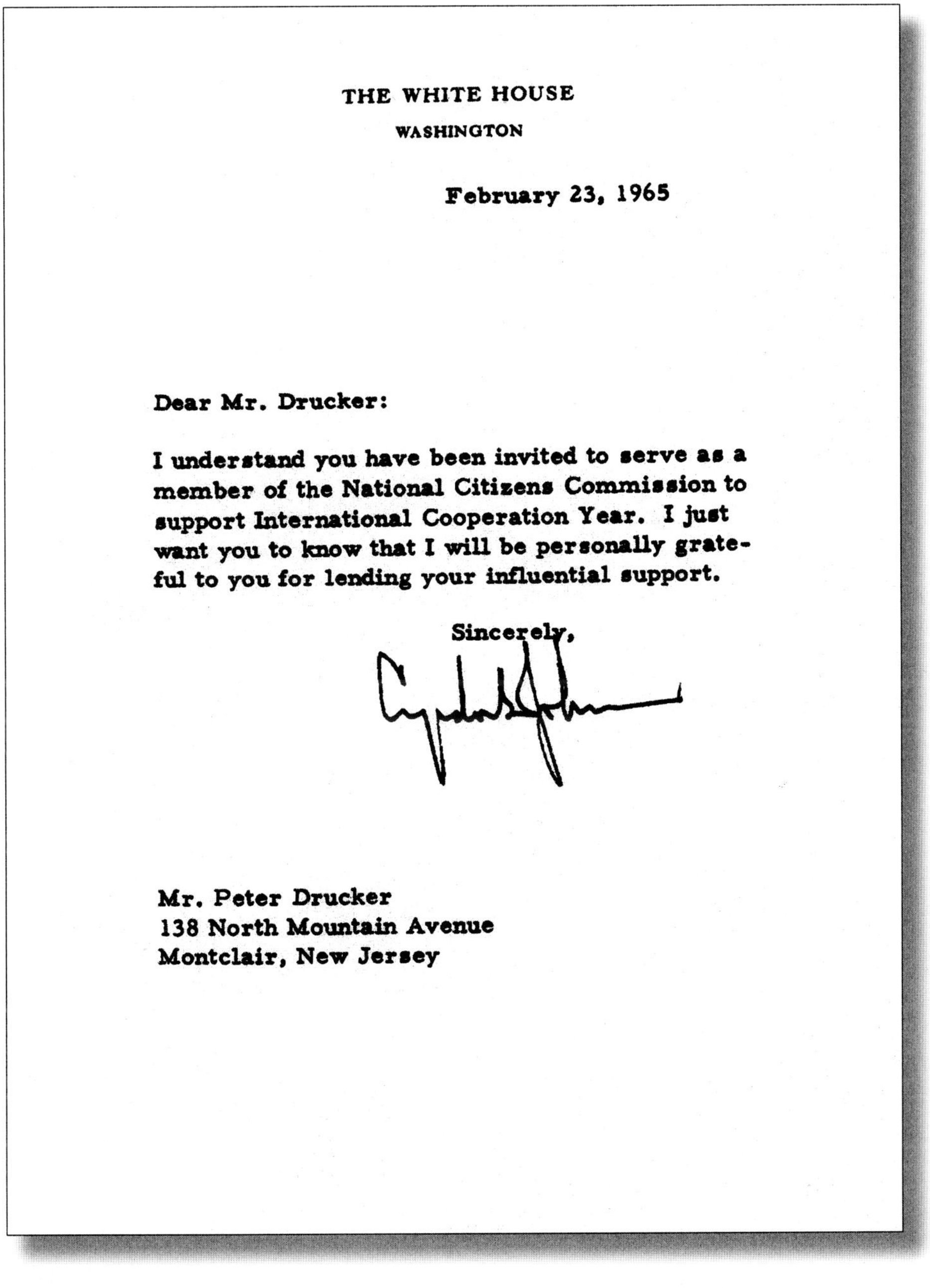

THE WHITE HOUSE

WASHINGTON

February 23, 1965

Dear Mr. Drucker:

I understand you have been invited to serve as a
member of the National Citizens Commission to
support International Cooperation Year. I just
want you to know that I will be personally grateful to you for lending your influential support.

Sincerely,

Mr. Peter Drucker
138 North Mountain Avenue
Montclair, New Jersey

July 12, 1960

MEMORANDUM

To: RN

From: Bob Finch

Enclosed is a series of three articles by this writer,
Peter Drucker, who Jim Worthy says is a former left-winger
who now wants to help in the cause. While I have had an
opportunity to read it, I understand his third article for
Harper's which is in galley proof form enclosed on the problem
of the Presidency, is worth reading.

Some of Richard Nixon's men may have been wary of Drucker's political leanings (or at least his "former" ones), as suggested by this 1960 memo from Nixon aide Bob Finch. Yet either way, as shown by the other note displayed here, Nixon made sure that Drucker's later views on "the sickness of government" were shared throughout his administration. Wrote Drucker: "There is mounting evidence that government is big rather than strong; that it is fat and flabby rather than powerful; that it costs a great deal but does not achieve much."

THE WHITE HOUSE

WASHINGTON

May 15, 1969

Dear Peter:

I think you would be interested to know that
the President has asked that your article in
The Public Interest, which I sent him a short
while ago, be reproduced and sent to all the
major members of his Administration with
the hope that they would find the time to give
it their careful attention.

Cordially,

Daniel P. Moynihan
Assistant to the President

Professor Peter Drucker
138 North Mountain Avenue
Montclair, New Jersey

Aside from Cold War madness, it's hard to imagine why the FBI ever opened a file on Drucker; pieces of that file are shown here. Drucker, after all, was no subversive. "Revolutions," he wrote, "cannot be predicted, directed, or controlled. They bring to power the wrong people. Worst of all, their results—predictably—are the exact opposite of their promises." Instead, Drucker wanted a society in which innovation flourished among all its institutions so that it could enjoy "self-renewal" without "bloodshed, civil war, or . . . economic catastrophe."

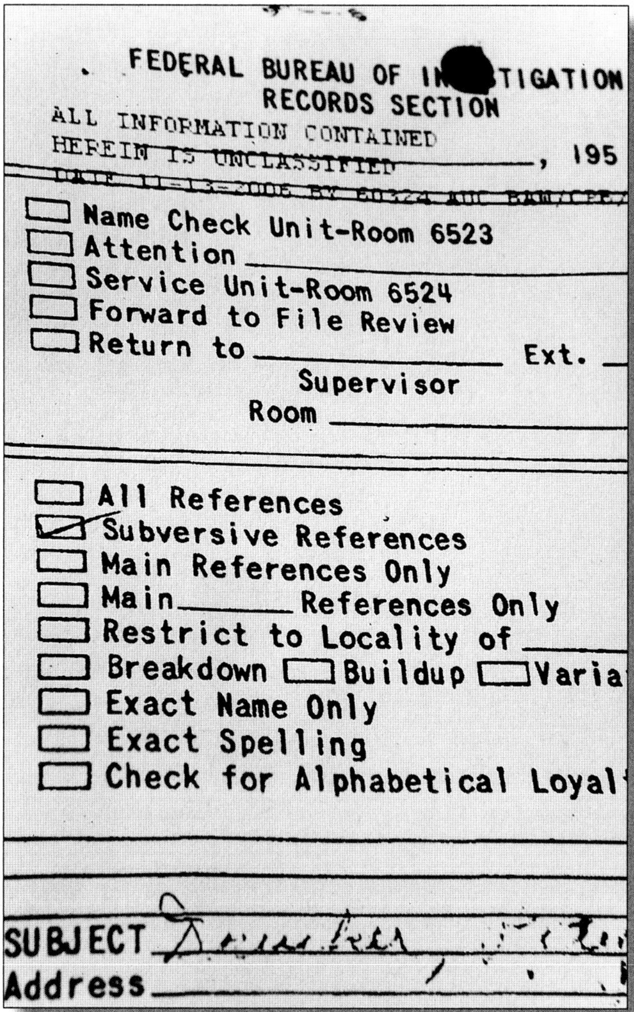

FEDERAL BUREAU OF INVESTIGATION
RECORDS SECTION
ALL INFORMATION CONTAINED
HEREIN IS UNCLASSIFIED _____, 195
DATE 11-13-2006 BY 60324 AUC BAW/CPB

☐ Name Check Unit-Room 6523
☐ Attention _____
☐ Service Unit-Room 6524
☐ Forward to File Review
☐ Return to _____ Ext. _
                 Supervisor
         Room _____

☐ All References
☑ Subversive References
☐ Main References Only
☐ Main_____ References Only
☐ Restrict to Locality of_____
☐ Breakdown ☐ Buildup ☐ Varia
☐ Exact Name Only
☐ Exact Spelling
☐ Check for Alphabetical Loyal

SUBJECT _Drucker_ _____
Address _____

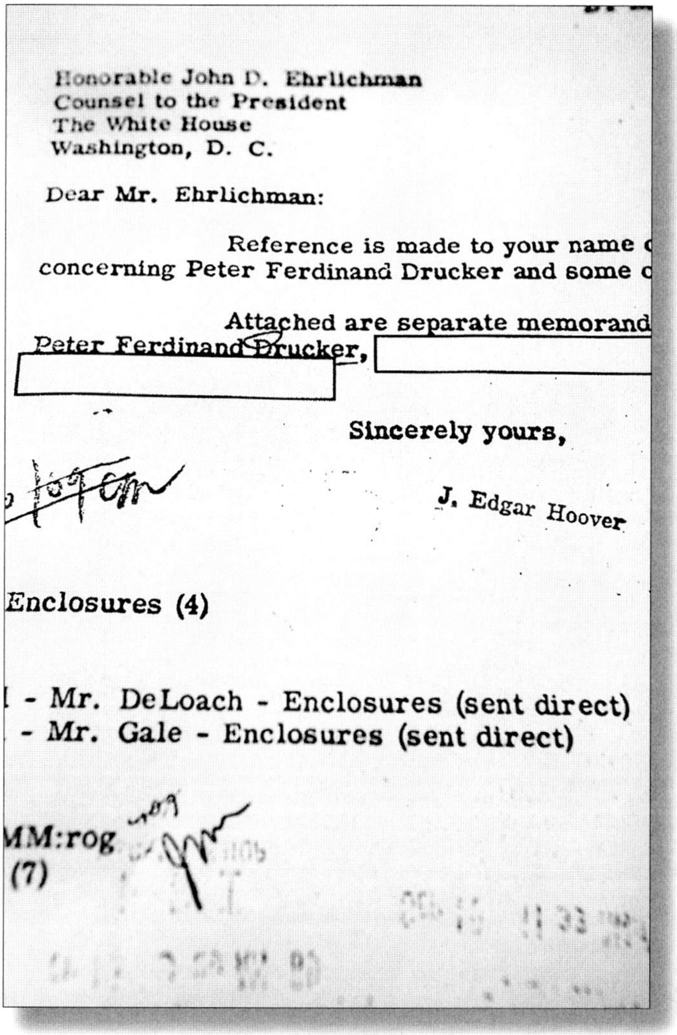

Honorable John D. Ehrlichman
Counsel to the President
The White House
Washington, D. C.

Dear Mr. Ehrlichman:

Reference is made to your name c
concerning Peter Ferdinand Drucker and some c

Attached are separate memorand
Peter Ferdinand Drucker,

Sincerely yours,

J. Edgar Hoover

Enclosures (4)

1 - Mr. DeLoach - Enclosures (sent direct)
 - Mr. Gale - Enclosures (sent direct)

MM:rog
(7)

February 4, 1976

Mr. Thomas D. Morris
Inspector General
Department of Health, Education and Welfare
Office of the Secretary
Washington, D.C. 20201

Dear Tom:

I am delighted to hear that you are still in the Government Service, and in such a crucial key job, at that. I had been wondering where you had gone — somebody told me that you had left GAO. I am really happy to hear that you have not chosen retirement yet; and that you are still willing to contribute to the public service and make available your unique knowledge, your unique skills and, above all, your tremendous personal integrity and leadership. This is wonderful news — and no agency needs you as badly as HEW. I only hope that you do occasionally take a little time off and enjoy life. I know the universe is in bad shape — but most of it, thank God, is in better shape than HEW.

I am also delighted to hear that you are presenting a paper on Bob McNamara, although — to my regret — I will not be there to hear you give it. I never attend a meeting in August — and altogether I do not attend meetings anymore. I concentrate my time on my own priority tasks of writing — a new book of mine is just about finished — teaching, consulting, and lecturing, in that order. And I try not to travel too much. By the way, i would strongly urge you to organize a top level federal government mission, I hope under your leadership, to the International Manage Congress (CIOS) in New Delhi this December. The Indians and the people in Asia altogether are launching a major effort and are working terribly hard to make this CIOS Congress a success. They do not have any money, of course — CIOS has no money, as you know, and India does not allow foreign exchange payments altogether. And so they would think, lest the United States will not be repaid at all. This, as you know, is not an organization

"The purpose of government is to focus the political energies of society," Drucker wrote. "It is to dramatize issues. It is to present fundamental choices. The purpose of government, in other words, is to govern. This, as we have learned in other institutions, is incompatible with 'doing.' Any attempt to combine government with 'doing' on a large scale paralyzes the decision-making capacity." Pictured here is a 1978 letter from Drucker commenting on the sad state of one federal agency, along with an invitation to the Reagan White House.

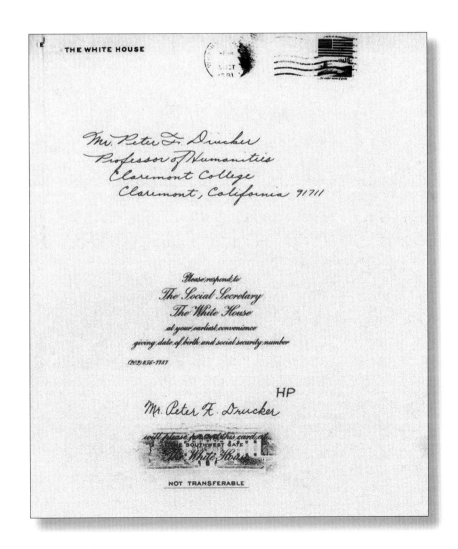

The Speaker
United States House of Representatives
Washington, D. C. 20515

Newt Gingrich
Sixth District
Georgia

6/28/96

To Peter Drucker

Thank you
For your Kind
remark about me as
an Entrepreneur. The
Effective Executive,
The Age of Discontinuities,
The Concept of the Corporation
and Management shaped
my practice of that art.

Your friend
Newt

NOT PRINTED AT GOVERNMENT EXPENSE

UNITED FARM WORKERS of AMERICA AFL-CIO
National Headquarters: La Paz, Keene, California 93531
(805) 822-5571

February 8, 1982

Mr. Peter F. Drucker
636 Wellesley Drive
Claremont, California 91711

Dear Mr. Drucker:

It was a pleasure to talk with you last week. I will
be looking forward to our meeting at 12:00 noon on
Thursday, February 18, 1982.

I may have one other person from our Executive Board
with me. I hope that will not be an inconvenience
for you.

Cordially,

Cesar E. Chavez
President

CEC:ew

2/18

Drucker said that he regarded himself "sometimes as a liberal
conservative and sometimes as a conservative liberal but
never as a 'conservative conservative' or a 'liberal liberal.'"
Perhaps this is why Drucker appealed to those from both ends
of the political spectrum. Among them: former GOP House
Speaker Newt Gingrich, who recommended that all members
of Congress read Drucker's *The Effective Executive*, and United
Farm Workers leader Cesar Chavez, whom Drucker advised on
immigration policy and other matters.

Peter Drucker receives his honorary Girl Scouts pin

The
Social-Sector
Advisor

Peter Drucker: In the last 20 years I have done a lot of work with the fast-growing pastoral churches. . . . And some of those people credit me . . . with having given them the key, the crucial concepts. And, of course, I've done a fair amount of common things, standing by, putting in my two-cents worth.

That's two cents adjusted for inflation, with a lot of institutions. I don't see any great difference between governments and the Girl Scouts and General Motors. They are very much alike.

Interviewer: Do you see one area between nongovernment organizations or educational institutions or anywhere else where you have had a greater effect than any other?

PD: Look, I probably have the greatest effect on nonprofits for the very elementary reason that for a long time I was the only one in there. I'm probably as well known among nonprofits as among businesses. . . . But I don't think that there is any area in which I've had an impact; there are individual people or individual companies where I've had an impact. Don't forget I have . . . never had the staff and never had employees or associates or partners. So the number of things I can handle at any one time is very small.

Drucker taught that the private sector hardly had a monopoly on exemplary management, a point that he made in his then-heretical 1989 *Harvard Business Review* article "What Business Can Learn from Nonprofits." The Salvation Army, in particular, impressed him. "No one even comes close to it with respect to clarity of mission, ability to innovate, measurable results, dedication, and putting money to maximum use," he said. Seen here is the Salvation Army's Evangeline Booth Award, given to Drucker in 2001, along with a commendation from the American Red Cross, where he also had a big impact.

The Social-Sector Advisor

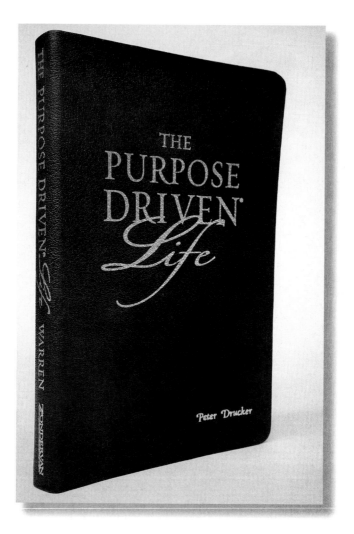

"The most significant sociological phenomenon of the first half of the twentieth century was the rise of the corporation," said Drucker. "The most significant sociological phenomenon of the second half of the twentieth century has been the development of the large pastoral church—of the mega-church." Pictured here is Drucker's personalized copy of *The Purpose Driven Life* by Pastor Rick Warren, who was close to Drucker for 20 years. Also shown is a paean to Drucker by Bob Buford, a social entrepreneur who has helped build the mega-church movement.

What Peter Drucker Does For Me

By Bob Buford June 14, 2002

1   He defines the landscape
    - What's behind, ahead, to each side (the context)
    - The social ecology in which my work plays a part
    - The futurity of present events
    - He creates new language ("knowledge worker")

2. He defines the opportunities, the void, what is needed <u>now</u>

3. He helps me to clarify my strengths and capacities
    - To build on strength
    - To avoid what I don't do well
    - To focus on making strengths productive
    - To identify the strengths of others that I need to be effective

4. He identifies the myths, the false paths, the incorrect assumptions of "the industry" within which I am working
    - What used to be true that no longer is
    - The conventional wisdom that will lead me astray

5   He encourages me to "go for it"
    - To commit myself and my funds to a new and needed project in an unfamiliar landscape
    - He gives me the insight, courage and confidence to go forward

6. He helps me to sort out the right strategies

7   He affirms results

8. He points out wasted effort
    - He helps me to stop doing things
    - "When the horse is dead, dismount"
    - When I have no results, he suggests that perhaps I don't know how to do it

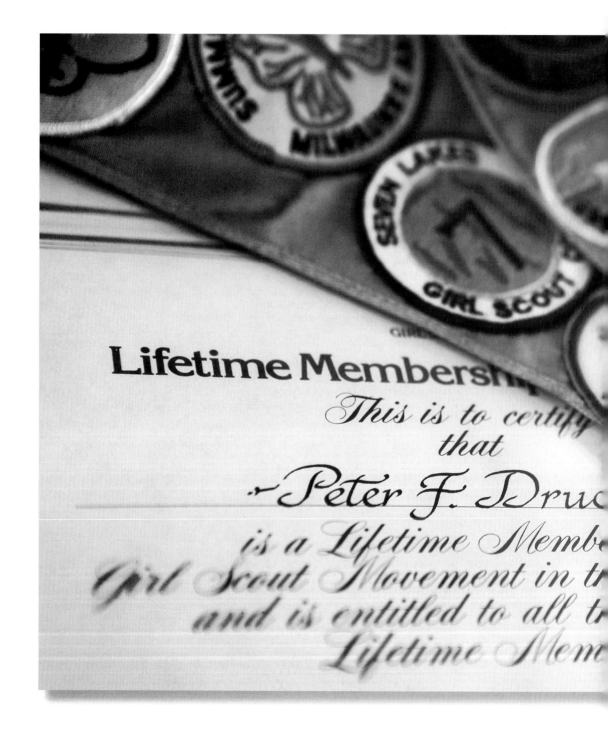

Girl Scouts CEO Frances Hesselbein—whom Drucker extolled as the best leader in the world, capable of running any corporation—had long been a close reader of *The Effective Executive* and other Drucker texts. In 1981, Drucker began consulting directly with the Girl Scouts, helping the staff answer five crucial questions and thereby transform scouting for a new era: What is our mission? Who is our customer? What does the customer value? What are our results? What is our plan? Shown here is Drucker's Girl Scouts sash and lifetime membership in the group.

Mutual of America

presents this

DISTINGUISHED CITIZENS SERVICE AWARD

to

Peter F. Drucker

We are pleased to pay special tribute to your eloquence as an educator and bestselling author. Your work has helped all of us to appreciate that not-for-profit institutions are central to American society and are indeed its most distinguishing feature.

We honor you, as the acknowledged "father of modern management", for the contribution you have made in the fields of economics, politics and social science. We also acknowledge with gratitude your significant contribution to the not-for-profit community, of which we are a part.

Your distinguished career as a professor of politics and philosophy has helped to revolutionize management both in theory and in practice.

It is a privilege to be associated with you and your noble work.

April 4, 1991

W. J. Flynn

Chairman and Chief Executive Officer

In Drucker's eyes, nonprofits are essential not only for what they do for the recipients of their services, but for the value and sense of fulfillment that they provide to their volunteers. "Citizenship in and through the social sector is not a panacea for the ills of . . . society," Drucker wrote, but it "restores the civic responsibility that is . . . the mark of community." Pictured here is a 1991 award from Mutual of America, honoring Drucker's work in the nonprofit arena, along with Drucker's personal list of community service activities.

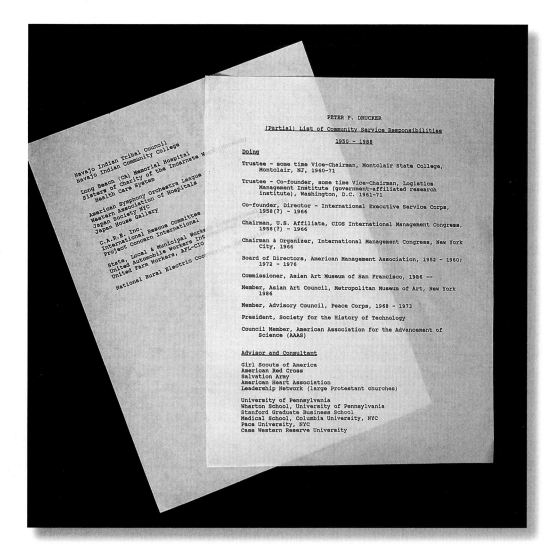

Navajo Indian Tribal Council
Navajo Indian Community College
Long Beach (CA) Memorial Hospital
Sisters of Charity of the Incarnate W
  Health Care System
American Symphony Orchestra League
Western Association of Hospitals
Japan Society NYC
Japan House Gallery
C.A.R.E. Inc.
International Rescue Committee
Project Concern International
State, Local & Municipal Worke
United Automobile Workers Int
United Farm Workers, AFL-CIO
National Rural Electric Coo'

PETER F. DRUCKER

(Partial) List of Community Service Responsibilities

1950 - 1988

Doing

Trustee - some time Vice-Chairman, Montclair State College, Montclair, NJ, 1960-71

Trustee - Co-founder, some time Vice-Chairman, Logistics Management Institute (government-affiliated research institute), Washington, D.C. 1961-71

Co-founder, Director - International Executive Service Corps, 1958(?) - 1966

Chairman, U.S. Affiliate, CIOS International Management Congress, 1958(?) - 1966

Chairman & Organizer, International Management Congress, New York City, 1966

Board of Directors, American Management Association, 1952 - 1960; 1972 - 1976

Commissioner, Asian Art Museum of San Francisco, 1986 --

Member, Asian Art Council, Metropolitan Museum of Art, New York 1986

Member, Advisory Council, Peace Corps, 1968 - 1973

President, Society for the History of Technology

Council Member, American Association for the Advancement of Science (AAAS)

Advisor and Consultant

Girl Scouts of America
American Red Cross
Salvation Army
American Heart Association
Leadership Network (large Protestant churches)

University of Pennsylvania
Wharton School, University of Pennsylvania
Stanford Graduate Business School
Medical School, Columbia University, NYC
Pace University, NYC
Case Western Reserve University

In 1999—long before the birth of the pro bono movement in America, in which businesses donate their employees' time and talent to the social sector—Drucker suggested another benefit of volunteering: it's a way for companies to develop their people. Nonprofits "are the places where the knowledge worker in an organization can actually discover who he is and can actually learn to manage himself or herself," Drucker said. Seen here is an award given to Drucker by CARE International, an organization dedicated to ending global poverty.

FIFTY

CARE

YEARS

CARE Foundation

International

Humanitarian Award

presented to

Peter F. Drucker

May 24, 1995
Los Angeles

Peter Drucker in Japan

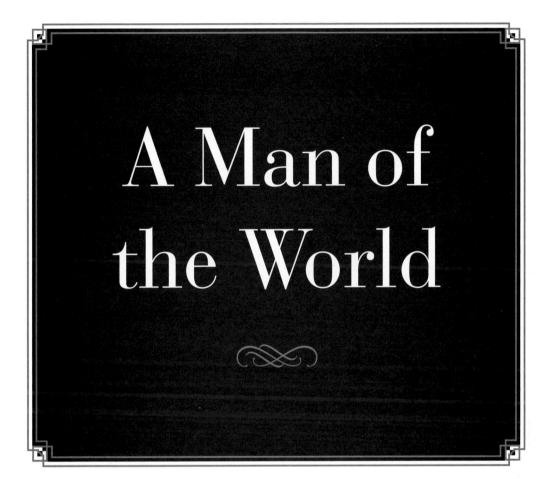

A Man of
the World

Interviewer: How did you first develop an interest in Japanese history and art?

Peter Drucker: June 7, 1934, 2:00 p.m., Saturday. I was working in a London bank. It was one of those glorious June days you can sometimes get in England, so I walked home, and we only worked till 12 o'clock on Saturday. It was a long walk home from the city to Hempstead, and halfway at Piccadilly Circus, a storm hit and I ducked into the first enclosed space, which was the Burlington Arcade. That's where the Royal Academy had its annual exhibition of paintings, and instead of its usual horrible paintings, there was their first travelling exhibition, the first exhibition of Japanese paintings. The Japanese government had sent them to the West. And I was hooked for life.

Thereafter, on my first trip to Japan, I began to—very gingerly at first—buy Japanese paintings. And then my wife joined me on my next trip, and she fell in love with Japan, too. . . . We began to collect a little more seriously. We made a serious mistake. We should have . . . broke the bank, borrowed everything we could borrow, and bought Japanese paintings in the sixties. Now we can't afford them.

Drucker: A Life in Pictures

In 2001, Drucker asked a successful businessman in Shanghai to name the most important thing that had happened in China in recent years. His response: "That we now consider owning an automobile a necessity and not a luxury." Concluded Drucker: "That is what globalization means. It is not an economic event; it's a psychological phenomenon" in which the "developed West's values . . . are seen as the norm." Shown here are a montage of postcards from Drucker's travels and a medal given to Drucker by the International Academy of Management.

Drucker, who first visited Japan in 1959, was among the first to predict the nation's rise to economic power. But he also became an expert in Japanese art. "The Japanese aesthetics are a way to understand . . . the very special (I would say unique) relationship between Japan and the outside world," he wrote. "It is a relationship based on receptivity . . . while at the same time accepting, or at least retaining, what makes Japan more Japanese." Seen here is Drucker's business card in Japanese, along with an award from the Emperor of Japan, bestowed in 1966.

ピーターF. ドラッカー
ニューヨーク大学経営学教授
クレアモンテ大学院大学社会科学特別教授

自宅：636 Wellesley Drive
Claremont, Cal. 91711
U. S. A.

Dr. Peter F.
of Management, Emeritus
School, Claremont Unive

日本国天皇は　アメリカ合衆国人

ピーター・フエルディナンド・ドラッカーを

勲三等に叙し瑞寶章を贈与する

昭和四十一年六月二十四日葉山において

璽をおさせる

第七九四七号

昭和四十一年六月二十四日

内閣総理大臣　佐藤榮作

総理府賞勲局長岩倉規夫

"变乃不变之永恒"。话虽如此，"变"也是内外皆变，内变更要靠人才与勇气。1997 年，三星聘请国外顶尖人才成立了战略应变小组，该智囊团由 25 位 MBA 人士组成，这些人均为世界顶尖学府出身的人士。每当三星集团遇到不便向外求助的难题时，该小组会立即集思广益，尽快制定相关战略并贯彻实施，直到问题解决。

德鲁克说："不创新，毋宁死（innovate or die）。"三星秉持着这种精神，因时而变，因势而变，不断追求创新。这种创新型的管理和创业式的经营，已成为三星企业文化的灵魂，就是以"变"为核心的新经营理念；以人才和技术为基础，创造最佳的产品和服务，为人类社会做贡献。其企业精神是"与顾客同在，向世界挑战，创造未来"。

三星集团确实体现出德鲁克创新的原则与精神，包括产品与服务的创新，市场、消费者行为和价值的创新，为制造产品与服务并将它们推出所需的各种技能与活动的创新。简而言之，就是产品创新、社会创新与管理创新。正因为如此，三星才成就了今日的三星。

三星集团现在是韩国最大的企业，也是韩国唯一进入全球品牌价值前 100 名的企业。2007 年

Among Drucker's core concepts—treating people as assets, acquiring the habit of effectiveness, and maintaining strong values—his insights on innovation have had particular resonance around the world. In South Korea, for example, many companies have turned to Drucker's ideas for what he termed "making tomorrow." Drucker, for his part, called Korea "undoubtedly" the most entrepreneurial nation on earth. Pictured here are Drucker's stark words "innovate or die" in Chinese, along with a stack of Drucker's books from across the globe.

"Technology and capital are simply tools," Drucker said. "They only become effective if properly used . . . by competent and effective management." With this in mind, the Beijing-based Peter F. Drucker Academy is training thousands of Chinese students a year in Drucker's principles. "You are not opening a university or business school of the traditional sense," Drucker told the academy's founder, Minglo Shao, "but you are trying to build a kind of new managerial culture." Pictured here is a ninety-fifth-birthday banner presented to Drucker by the academy.

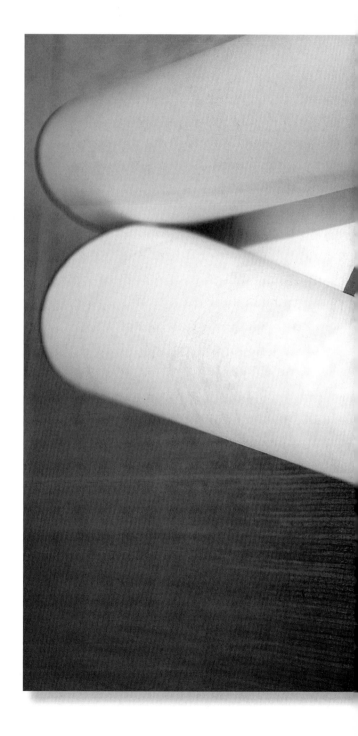

BOMBAY MANAGEMENT ASSOCIATIO

Honorary Membership

YOU, PETER FERDINAND DRUCKER, through your teachings, writings and consulting services over a span of four decades, have caused a total revolution in the thinking and practice of management. You have endeared yourself to the hearts of the world's managers, made them understand the role and place of management as one among the learned disciplines and given them a sense of status and function in society. Through your books and writings, teaching and counselling, you have undoubtedly become their Mentor. You have enabled them to make your messages their own in the practice of the art and craft of Management.

We in the developing countries, especially in India and more specifically, in the Bombay Management Association ever since we banded ourselves into a professional body barely twelve to sixteen have always admired and benefitted from your phenomenal contributions to management knowledge and practice which had always had prac...
and manage...

In recognition and grateful...
numerous other accomplishment...
of the wellbeing of the poo...
management, we take great...
HONORARY MEMBERSHIP...
Association with all the rol...
By accepting this Honorary Me...
its your graceful and perman...
...we carry on the miss...

"India and China are very rapidly becoming counterforces to American economic dominance," Drucker told a class in 2003. "These are two very different countries. They are both emerging into the world economy as great . . . powers but quite differently. China is a manufacturing center. India is a knowledge center." Seen here is a plaque from 1978 touting Drucker's honorary membership in the Bombay Management Association, along with the manuscript for the Chinese edition of Drucker's *A Functioning Society*.

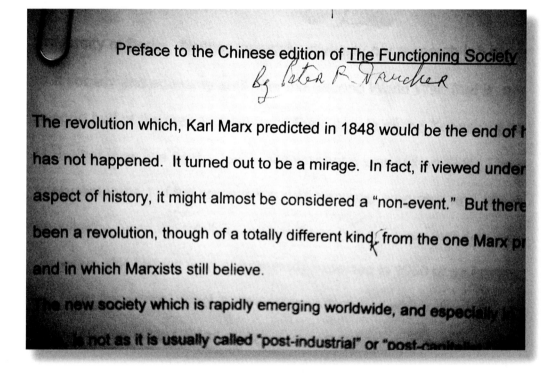

Preface to the Chinese edition of <u>The Functioning Society</u>

By Peter F. Drucker

The revolution which, Karl Marx predicted in 1848 would be the end of h

has not happened. It turned out to be a mirage. In fact, if viewed under

aspect of history, it might almost be considered a "non-event." But there

been a revolution, though of a totally different kind, from the one Marx p

and in which Marxists still believe.

he new society which is rapidly emerging worldwide, and especially

not as it is usually called "post-industrial" or "post-cap

Drucker's books have been published in more than 40 languages, and Drucker Societies, a loose network of volunteers who bring about positive change in their local communities by delivering a variety of programs built on Drucker's teachings, have emerged across the globe. Here one can get a sense of Drucker's extensive reach, from Bolivia (where Drucker was made an "honorary admiral" in 1989) to the Balkans (with special birthday greetings from the Macedonian capital of Skopje).

USIS SKOPJE

UNITED STATES INFORMATION SERVICE
GRADSKI ZID, BLOK IV • 91000 SKOPJE
TELEPHONE (389)(91) 116 623, 117 129
FAX (389)(91) 118 431

E-MAIL USISSKP@LOTUS.MK

GREETING CARD TO PETER DRUCKER

PETER F. DRUCKER
DEPT. OF MANAGEMENT
CLAREMONT GRADUATE SCHOOL
170 E. 10TH ST
CLAREMONT, CA 91711-6163

DEAR PROFESSOR DRUCKER,

ON THE OCCASION OF YOUR BIRTHDAY, WE ORGANIZED A ROUND TABLE
IN SKOPJE -- THE CAPITAL OF THE FORMER YUGOSLAV REPUBLIC OF
MACEDONIA, HEADLINED: "PETER DRUCKER - VISIONARY AND CREATOR."

OUR GOAL WAS, THROUGH REAFFIRMATION OF YOUR IDEAS IN THESE
AREAS, TO TRY TO SOLVE SOME OF THE PROBLEMS FACING OUR
COUNTRY.

THUS, THAT THE UNIVERSALITY OF YOUR WORK KNOWS NO GEOGRAPHICAL
OR POLITICAL BOUNDARIES IS CONFIRMED AGAIN. SIMPLY STATED,
YOUR WORK IS BECOMING A TREASURE TO ALL OF THOSE WHO LOVE TO
THINK.

HAPPY BIRTHDAY, WITH SINCERE WISHES FOR LONG LIFE AND GOOD
HEALTH. IN RETURN, WE ARE HOPING TO ENRICH OUR KNOWLEDGE WITH
SOME NEW WORK FROM YOU.

ORGANIZERS OF THE ROUND TABLE:

  - EKO PRESS ECONOMY MAGAZINE
  - COPIS - NT PRIVATE ENTERPRISE
  - U.S. INFORMATION SERVICE/SKOPJE

PARTICIPANTS IN THE ROUND TABLE:

  - RETIRED AND ACTIVE PROFESSORS FROM "SV. KIRIL AND METODIJ
UNIVERSITY"
  - STUDENTS
  - BUSINESSMEN

Peter Drucker in his Kansas City Royals garb

Family Man, Friend, and Fan

Interviewer: What I think I'm hearing from you . . . is that one needs to look at one's total life—one's family, friends, one's various organizations—and perhaps not be too focused on one thing.

Peter Drucker: I wouldn't say "happy people," but the satisfied, contented people I knew . . . lived in more than one world. Those single-minded people—you meet them most in politics—in the end are very unhappy people. There isn't that much room at the top. And you rarely last very long at the top.

The number of people who really like to be at the top—which means that you don't eat dinner at home more than once a week, which means that your children have to wear name tags—I've known them. And the contented . . . people I've known are people who make a life that has more than one dimension so that if you are set back in one area, it doesn't kill you.

D 804296

CERTIFIED COPY of an
Pursuant to the Marriage

ENT

Act

Registration District   HAMPSTEAD

1937.   Marriage Solemnized at   *The Register Office*

District of _____   HAMPSTEAD   in the   METROPOLIT
OF HAM

Columns:—	1	2	3	4	5
No.	When Married.	Name and Surname.	Age.	Condition.	Rank or Profession.
111	Sixteenth January 1937	Peter Georg Drucker	27 Years	Bachelor	Bank Manager
		Doris Schmitz	25 Years	Spinster	

Married in the _The Register Office_ ~~according to the Rites and Ceremoni~~

This Marriage was solemnized between us, { Peter Drucker Doris Schmitz } in the Presence of us, { W. G. Halpern Ella Berg }

I, Edward Best , Registrar of Marriages for the District of   HAM
now legally in my custody.   do hereby certify that this is a true copy of the Entry No. 111   in th

WITNESS MY HAND this 16th day of January 1

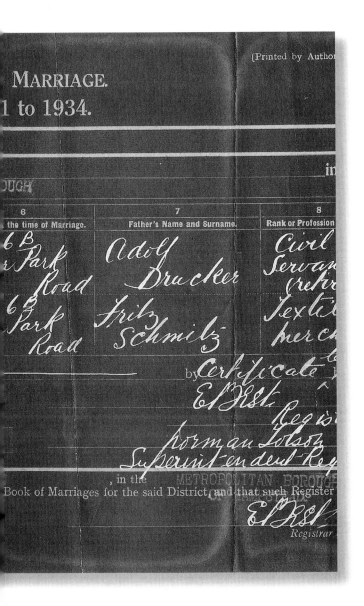

MARRIAGE.

1 to 1934.

Drucker's wife, Doris, a German native, served as Peter's unofficial editor for the 71 years they were married. She had studied economics and law in Europe and then earned a master's degree in physics from Fairleigh Dickinson University. Just like her husband's, Doris's intellectual curiosity knows no bounds. In her acclaimed autobiography, *Invent Radium or I'll Pull Your Hair*, she reflects on the work of Goethe: "What . . . puzzles me, is this: How can you become an educated person without reading these books?" Shown here is the Druckers' marriage certificate.

At age 82, Doris Drucker started a company that manufactured an electronic device to warn speakers in large lecture halls if their voice dropped too low for everyone to hear. Although the business was born of Doris's shouting, "Louder!" to Peter during his speeches, he had little to do with the company. "He watched it happen with great astonishment," Doris said. "Peter does my taxes—and I bless him for that—but he has no idea about building start-ups." Seen here is a love note from Doris to Peter, along with a drawing of the family by one of their four children.

Drucker maintained friendships with other luminaries in the fields of management and economics. Among them was Austrian native Karl Polanyi, author of *The Great Transformation*, whose work emphasized the way in which economies are embedded in society and culture. Drucker also counted as a friend W. Edwards Deming, the statistician who is widely considered the father of modern quality control and whose teachings helped boost Japanese industry after World War II. Shown here are letters from Drucker to both Polanyi and Deming.

PETER F. DRUCKER
BENNINGTON COLLEGE
BENNINGTON, VERMONT

February 9, 1949

Dr.Karl Polanyi.
423 West 120th Street
New York,N.Y.

Dear Karl:

The Pittsburgh deal,alas, fell through at the very last moment - in fact, after the last moment so to speak. Indeed, it was too good to be true, and I would have been very much more dubious about it had the Dean not assured me that he had full approval from his various authorities so that the ratification of the appointment was a mere formaŀlity, something which turned out to have been a very rash statement, to say the least. I am annoyed by the loss of time to look around, especially as January is the best academic hunting month, but not otherwise depressed as the development clearly shows that Pittsburgh, in spite of all its promises, would not have been willing or politically able to back me in a program which would undoubtedly provoke the opposition of powerful local forces, especially in management.

I write you this both because I want to keep you posted and because I wonder whether your careful research into the Columbia Business School situation has brought any results. I also want to tell you that I am definitely not continuing at Bennington. I shall go on sabbatical leave at the end of this academic year from which I will not return here - something which, as I know, will not surprise you.

The book is making very good progress. I feel gay and light-hearted about it for the first time. I still do not want to show you anything till I have a reasonably even draft of the whole. But I feel now that this will be the case within another three months.

May I also remind you of your half-promise to come up here during midterm or at the latest during the Easter vacations ? We want to present Joan Agatha to you and we all very much want to see you.

With all our love,

Peter

PETER F DRUCKER
636 WELLESLEY DRIVE
CLAREMONT CALIFORNIA 91711
TELEPHONE: (714) 621 1488

May 19, 1976

Professor W. Edwards Deming
Graduate School of Business Administration
New York University
100 Trinity Place
New York, New York   10006

Dear Ed:

I am unhappy that I cannot join with all your GBA friends
at this reception to honor you at your retirement. I am
too far away and will not be able to attend. But I do
not want to let this occasion go by without conveying
to you my very warmest wishes. You already were one
of the stars and leaders at GBA when I joined the faculty
in 1950. And from the beginning, I looked to you and
to a few of the other seniors of the time for inspiration,
for guidance, and above all for standards. What I have
learned from your example is beyond measurement – and
cannot possibly be sampled, not even unscientifically.
But the example you gave all of us – in your concern
for the individual student; in your kindness towards
the new and young faculty member; and in your complete
uncompromising integrity of standards and insistence
on principle – was inspiration, guidance, and a constant
source of renewal for me and of pride in being privileged
to be associated with you.

And so I am joining with all your friends, students
and admirers today in wishing you the very best for
your retirement – I know it will be an active one,
a productive one, and I hope a healthy and a very long
one. If only I were good enough to write a Canticle
of Praise and Thanksgivings for William Edwards Deming.

In old friendship,

As always, yours,

Perhaps more than any other item in the Drucker Archives, this 1972 missive from Drucker to two old friends sheds light on what Drucker's day-to-day life as a writer, teacher, consultant, father, and husband was like. In the letter, Drucker notes that he had

PETER F. DRUCKER
636 WELLESLEY DRIVE
CLAREMONT, CALIFORNIA 91711
TELEPHONE: (714) 621-1488

July 25, 1972

Dear Jim, dear Millie,

First our very warmest wishes on the new homes and on the new assignment. I hope Jim enjoys Sangamon State (if not, he has only himself to blame-- he invented the place, after all).

As you will see from this letterhead we too have moved-- we moved a year and a half ago. We did not, however, try to set up two residences though we flirted with the idea. (and anyhow we do have a summer home in the Colorado Rockies where we spend two months each year, as a rule, as you know). Rather we looked for a year-round climate and for the work base to go with it. I considered Stanford but they wanted me to be a full-time academician and to take on a lot of educational chores- they have never intrigued me. So I accepted appointment as Clarke Research Professor of Social Science at Claremont Graduate School-- one of the Claremont Colleges (of which Pomona is the oldest and best known) thirty miles East of Los Angeles on the foot of lovely high mountains. I have known these colleges for many years and am very fond of them. And I have no more teaching than one day a week- the teaching load I have been carrying for many years. I have agreed to stay on officially on the NYU faculty as a Distinguish-ed University Professor; but that means three lectures a year- public ones- usually in April when I have to be in New York anyhow.

Otherwise I keep on the work I have been doing all along. Or rather I am slowly changing a little bit. Instead of 100 days of consulting - this last year it was 135 which is too much- I'll cut outside consulting and lecturing slowly back to 45 or 50 days, retaining primar-ily the clients I am most interested in. But at the same time I have been serving as the main editorial advisor to the Saturday Review Magazines after a group of my friends acquired them from the former editor and publisher who almost killed them off through gross non-management. And beginning this coming September we are (a) moving these magazines out of New York and to San Francisco, and (b) I'll officially (though we may not announce it) take over as Chairman of the Editorial Advisory Board which would mean five days a month, ten months a year in San Francisco-- since two of our four children live there anyhow, this is totally acceptable to us. Indeed we may, in a year or two, move up to San Francisco-- though we enjoy the Los Angeles Sun and especially the daily swim, first thing in the morning- after which I'd commute one day a week during the academic year to Claremont, keeping a faculty apartment there but living in the San Francisco area--we haven't made up our mind and will try commuting to San Francisco first. So I am busier than ever-- and on top of this I am deep into a new book. I started a year and a half ago to revise PRACTICE OF MANAGEMENT-- it came out

tried to update his 1954 classic *The Practice of Management*, but "I soon found that I couldn't 'update' but had to write an entirely new—and, alas, monstrously long—book." *Management: Tasks, Responsibilities, Practices* was published the next year.

PETER F. DRUCKER

in 1954 and shows its age even though it is still the best seller . I soon found that I couldn t " update" but had to write an entirely new- and, alas , monstrously long- book. I am about two thirds or more through- though I have been saying this for almost a year now. I still hope to have it finished by the end of the year but know that this is unlikely-- it will be next Spring. Piled on top of all the other things I'm doing (and my consulting has become predominantly public-service institutions such as the L.A. County School System (a mess) and the City of Los Angeles (also a mess), I am far busier than I've ever been. I know I have to cut back-but so far I am piling on.

Doris is also working very hard-- you may remember that she is a physicist and that she qualified a few years back as a Registered Patent Agent. And since we have been to Japan a great deal - our youngest daughter, Joan, is there now finishing a graduate year after which she'll go to Chicago next year to get her Master's- and since Doris is industrious (I am lazy) and learned Japanese, at least to read, she has become the U.S. correspondent for the leading Japanese patent lawyers and their representative in getting Japanese patents re-done and patented under U.S. laws. She too, instead of slowing down, has speeded up. But it seems to be good for us. At least we are hiking and climbing more every year- this year in particular. And we do get time off for travelling together-- we were in Japan last May/June, for instance-- our ninth tenth trip in twelve years, by the way.

Our children are all over the map. Kathleen, the oldest, is married in Boston- to an MIT designer-planner. She has two small boys. And her first major book of poetry is just about to be published by Doubleday-- she has become one of the better-known young poets. Our son Vincent is just about to launch a magazine - for the class room teacher- on which he has been working for three years. He has now raised all the money, has the staff and will bring out the first issue in October. He lives in San Francisco, as does Cecily, our second daughter who after a highly successful career as a banker (she was vice preseident of a Bank of America subsidiary) decided to do what she should have done all along, that is go to law school- she just finished her first year and is blissfully happy. A nd Joan, the youngest, just finished two and a half years in Japan. After graduating in Japanese studies she first taught English in a school in Japan andthen took her first year graduate work in Tokyo- she'll fin- ish up at Chicago next year.

And how about Carol, her husband and her children.

Again all our best- and we'd like to see you when you ever get out to the West Coast

as always

Drucker studied musical composition as a youngster and considered taking it up full time. Although his career turned elsewhere, he often looked to music for lessons that could be applied to management. "To build a world-class orchestra requires rehearsing the same passage in the symphony again and again until the first clarinet plays it the way the conductor hears it," Drucker wrote in *Harvard Business Review*. "This principle is also what makes a research director in an industry lab successful." Pictured here are some of Drucker's favorite albums from his personal collection.

Drucker called himself a "very old environmentalist," noting that he had offered a course on ecology in the late 1940s at Bennington College. Nobody signed up. "It seemed a very strange and wildly reactionary notion at that time that we have to make sure of not destroying too much of the natural inheritance of man," Drucker explained. He himself loved to hike and climb, and he did so, often yodeling as he went, from Mount Fuji in Japan to the peaks of Colorado. Seen here is one of Drucker's walking sticks, along with some edelweiss picked up during one of his treks.

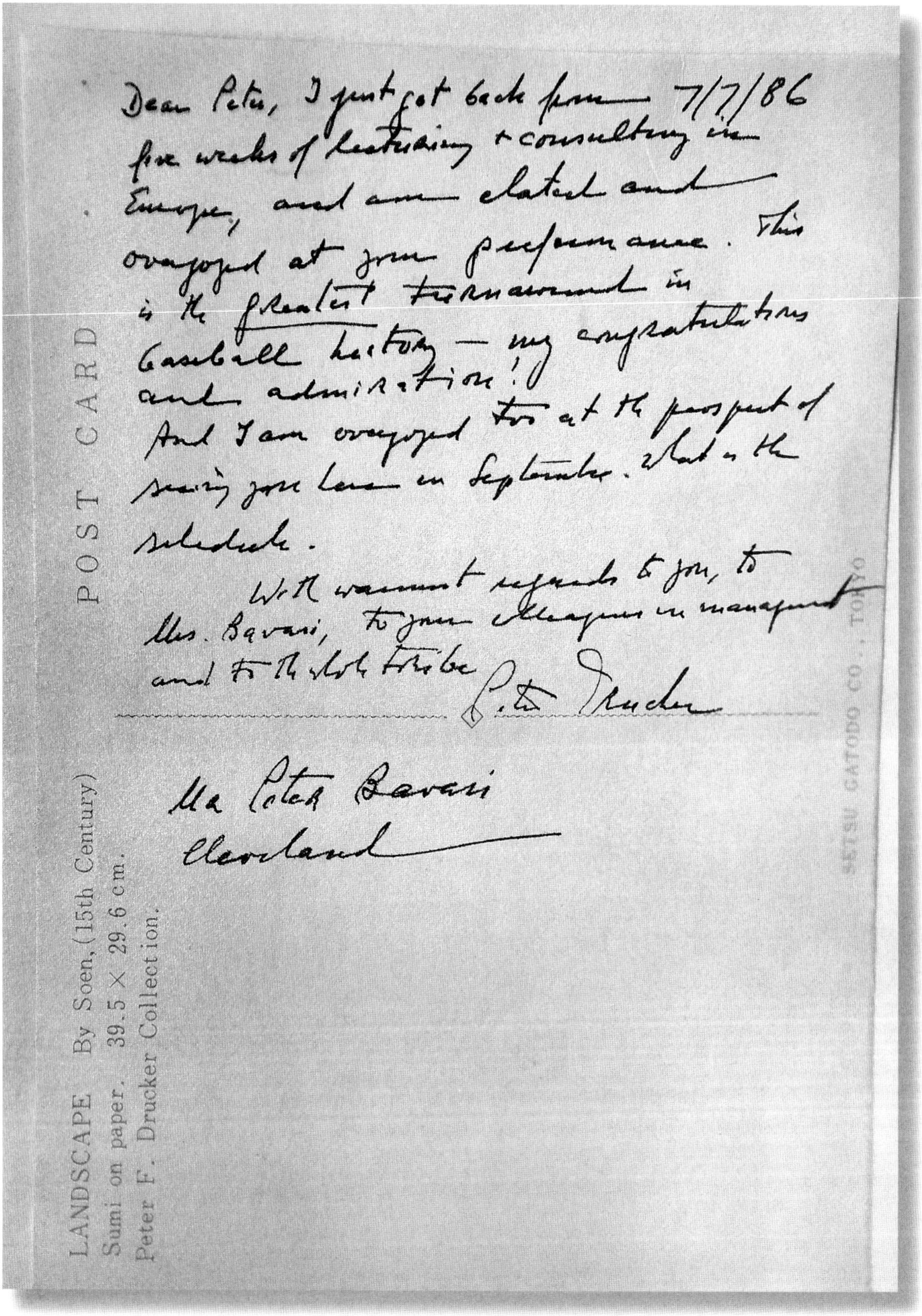

POST CARD

Dear Peter, I just got back from 7/7/86 five weeks of lecturing & consulting in Europe, and am elated and overjoyed at your performance. This is the greatest turnaround in baseball history — my congratulations and admiration! And I am overjoyed too at the prospect of seeing you here in September. What is the schedule.

With warmest regards to you, to Mrs. Bavasi, to your colleagues in management and to the whole tribe

Peter Drucker

Mr. Peter Bavasi
Cleveland

SETSU GATODO CO., TOKYO

LANDSCAPE   By Soen, (15th Century)
Sumi on paper.   39.5 × 29.6 cm.
Peter F. Drucker Collection.

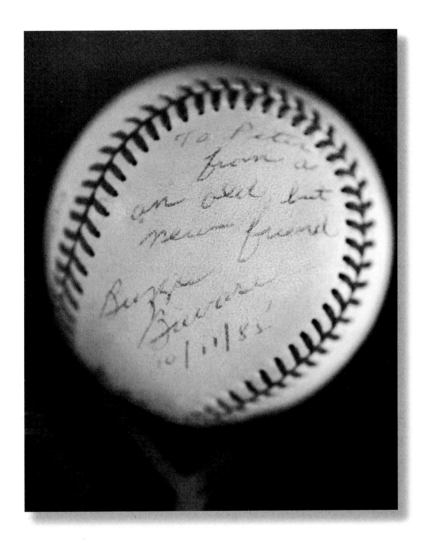

The Druckers didn't own a TV, but Peter would rent a set so that he could watch one event a year: the World Series. In 1986, he advised the Cleveland Indians, helping the club's president, Peter Bavasi, implement Drucker's famous system of Management by Objectives. The results were dazzling: the team won 84 games, up from only 60 the previous season. Shown here is Drucker's note to Bavasi, congratulating him on the turnaround. Also pictured is a baseball from Bavasi's father, Buzzie, who had been general manager of the Dodgers.

MAX O. DE PREE
2967 LAKESHORE DR.
HOLLAND, MI 49424

2/13/98

Dear Peter,
    I have thoroughly enjoyed Jack Beatty's new book. I hope you feel good about it.
    It's been good for me to review—through Beatty's elegant prose—so many of the ideas, concepts and experiences I have heard from you over so many years.
    I am especially grateful for his clear grasp of your beliefs and values which for me have been powerfully supportive.

In a nicely unemba[rrassing] way he gives his rea[der] glimpses of the dept[h] breadth of your tea[ching] which those of us [who] know you well are — [some]times tempted to ta[ke] for granted.
    I am giving a cop[y to] each of our children partly for a selfish re[ason] Mr. Beatty refers to [you as] your friend. Of cour[se,] many years and at c[ertain] moments you've bee[n my] teacher and mento[r for] which I will alwa[ys] be indebted.

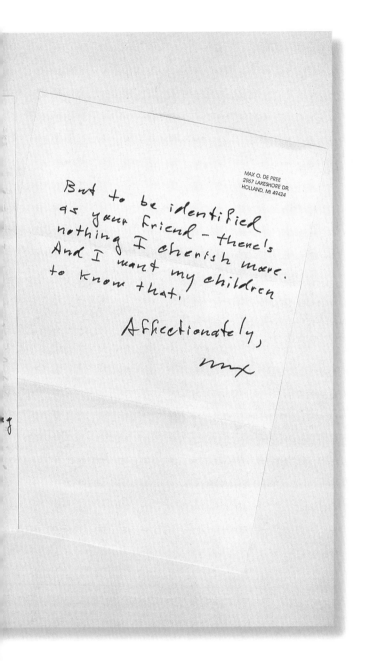

But to be identified as your friend — there's nothing I cherish more. And I want my children to know that.

Affectionately,

max

MAX O. DE PREE
2967 LAKESHORE DR.
HOLLAND, MI 49424

Max De Pree, the former CEO of furniture maker Herman Miller, drew on Drucker's teachings in his book *Leadership Is an Art*. "Leaders are responsible for effectiveness," De Pree said. "Much has been written about effectiveness—some of the best of it by Peter Drucker. He has such a great ability to simplify concepts. One of the things he tells us is that efficiency is doing the thing right, but effectiveness is doing the right thing." Yet as this letter makes clear, De Pree valued Drucker as more than a teacher; above all, he valued him as a friend.

Peter Drucker receives the Presidential Medal of Freedom

The
Drucker
Legacy

Interviewer: Peter Drucker, I have a final question, and I hope you will humor me and not consider me too greedy.

You've lived a long life and focused intensely on life and how it's lived. Now you're 95. What about an afterlife? What about God? How do you think about the moment of transition that you are inevitably approaching?

Peter Drucker: Well, I happen to be a very conventional, traditional Christian. Period. And I don't think about it. I am told. It's not my job to think about it. My job is to say, "Yes, Sir."

Interviewer: That must be very comforting.

PD: It is, and I say every morning and every evening, "Praise be to God for the beauty of His creation. Amen."

In 2002, three years before he died, Drucker was awarded the Presidential Medal of Freedom, the nation's highest civilian honor. At the White House ceremony, Drucker was lauded for his "groundbreaking insights," which "have helped many business, government, and nonprofit organizations to succeed." His writings, it was noted, have "significantly influenced the shape of our society." Seen here is Drucker's Medal of Freedom, along with a list of what he considered his greatest contributions to the discipline of management.

636 WELLESLEY DRIVE
CLAREMONT CALIFORNIA 91711
TELEPHONE: (909) 621-1488
FAX: (909) 626-7366

January 18, 1999

What do I consider my most important Contributions?

- That I early on— almost sixty years ago- realized that MANAGEMENT
  has become the constitutive organ and function of the <u>Society</u>
  <u>of Organizations</u> ;

- That MANAGEMENT is not "Business Management- though it first attained
  attention in business- but the governing organ of ALL institutions of
  Modern Society;

- That I established the study of MANAGEMENT as a DISCIPLINE in its own right;

  and

- That I focused this discipline on People and Power; on Values; Structure and
  Constitution; AND ABOVE ALL ON RESPONSIBILITIES- that is focused the
  <u>Discipline of Management</u> on Management as a truly LIBERAL ART.

  Peter F. Drucker

As he neared the end of his long life, a close friend asked Drucker how he wanted to be remembered. "I am a writer," Drucker replied. "My legacy is my writing. I did not create an institution. Now, what do you want to talk about?" Pictured here is Drucker's complete oeuvre—more than 10,000 book pages in all—as seen on a shelf at the Drucker Institute in Claremont. Most stunning, perhaps, is that Drucker wrote two-thirds of these books after he'd reached his mid-sixties, a time when most people retire.

Despite Drucker's retort that "I did not create an institution," two institutions continue to build on his work. In 2004, the Drucker School of Management was renamed the Peter F. Drucker and Masatoshi Ito Graduate School of Management in honor of its new benefactor, a prominent Japanese businessman and a friend of Drucker's. In 1998, the Drucker Archives was created; in 2006, it became part of the newly formed Drucker Institute. Seen here are a video from the dedication for the Drucker-Ito School and a program from the archives' inauguration.

Claremont Graduate University
Peter F. Drucker Graduate School of
Management

Inauguration of the Peter F. Drucker Archives
and Research Library
May 15, 1998

In 2009 and 2010, the Drucker Centennial was held in honor of the 100th anniversary of Drucker's birth. It featured conferences, lectures, and other events all over the world. Seen here is the block just outside the Drucker School and Institute; it was renamed Drucker Way, from Eleventh Street, as part of the centennial. Also shown is the ceiling at the institute, where a steady stream of Twitter feeds referring to the institute's work is projected. The tweets serve as a constant reminder to the staff that, as Drucker taught, "all the results are on the outside."

Photo Permissions and Credits

*Originals of all documents can be found in the Drucker Archives,
except the following, which are being used by permission:*

Student ID card, p. 10
Goethe-University Frankfurt am Main, University Archives.

"Nobody . . . has heard of Drucker" letter, p. 16
Emergency Committee in Aid of Displaced Foreign Scholars,
Manuscripts and Archives Division, New York Public Library.

Irving Kristol letter, p. 17
Irving Kristol Papers, Wisconsin Historical Society Archives.

Table of contents for *Management*, p. 26
Harper & Row, Publishers records, 1935–1973, Columbia
University Libraries.

Lyndall Urwick letter, p. 28
Lyndall Urwick Archive, Henley Business School, University of
Reading.

"Elton Mayo" letter, p. 29
Ronald Greenwood Papers, Nova Southeastern University
Archives.

The Recent Future letter, p. 36
John Sylvester Fischer Papers. Manuscripts and Archives, Yale University Library.

"Never . . . any desire to become an editor" letter, p. 38
Melvin Kranzberg Papers, Archives Center, National Museum of American History, Smithsonian Institution.

1940 "classroom abilities" letter, p. 46
"A Guide to the Papers of the Institute of Public Affairs," University of Virginia, 1927-1953, Special Collections, University of Virginia Library.

Richard Jenrette letter, p. 66
Richard H. Jenrette Papers, Southern Historical Collection, Wilson Library, University of North Carolina at Chapel Hill.

Bob Finch memo, p. 82
Vice Presidential files, Richard Nixon Presidential Library and Museum.

Karl Polanyi letter, p. 128
Karl Polanyi Archive.

W. Edwards Deming letter, p. 129
W. Edwards Deming Papers, Manuscript Division, Library of Congress.

All interview excerpts are from an oral history with Peter Drucker conducted for the Drucker Archives on August 26, 1999, by Amy Donnelly, except the following:

"The Immigrant" interview excerpt, p. 5
Big Picture Media Corporation, undated, transcript, Drucker Archives.

"The Business Consultant" interview excerpt, p. 61

"Family Man, Friend, and Fan" interview excerpt, p. 123
By Bruce Rosenstein, April 11, 2005, transcript, Drucker Archives.

"The Drucker Legacy" interview excerpt, p. 143
By Tom Ashbrook, "On Point with Tom Ashbrook," National Public Radio, August 2, 2005.

About
Peter F. Drucker

Born in Vienna, Austria, in 1909, Peter F. Drucker was a writer, professor, management consultant, and self-described "social ecologist," who explored the way human beings organize themselves and interact much the way an ecologist would observe and analyze the biological world.

Hailed by *BusinessWeek* as "the man who invented management," Drucker directly influenced a huge number of leaders from a wide range of organizations across all sectors of society. Among the many: the White House, General Electric, IBM, Intel, Procter & Gamble, Girl Scouts of the USA, the Salvation Army, Red Cross, and the United Farm Workers.

Drucker's 39 books, along with his countless scholarly and popular articles, predicted many of the major developments of the late twentieth century, including privatization and decentralization, the rise of Japan to economic world power, the decisive importance of marketing and innovation, and the emergence of the information society with its necessity of lifelong learning. In the late 1950s, Drucker coined the term "knowledge worker," and he spent the rest of his life examining an age in which an unprecedented number of people use their brains more than their backs.

Throughout his work, Drucker called for a healthy balance—between short-term needs and long-term sustainability; between profitability and other obligations; between the specific mission of individual organizations and the common good; between freedom and responsibility.

Drucker's first major work, *The End of Economic Man*, was published in 1939. After reading it, Winston Churchill described Drucker as "one of those writers to whom almost anything can be forgiven because he not only has a mind of his own, but has the gift of starting other minds along a stimulating line of thought."

Driven by an insatiable curiosity about the world around him—and a deep desire to make that world a better place—Drucker continued to write long after most others would have put away their pens. The result was a ceaseless procession of landmarks and classics: *Concept of the Corporation* in 1946, *The Practice of Management* in 1954, *The Effective Executive* in 1967, *Management: Tasks, Responsibilities, Practices* in 1973, *Innovation and Entrepreneurship* in 1985, *Post-Capitalist Society* in 1993, *Management Challenges for the 21st Century* in 1999.

Drucker, who had taught at Sarah Lawrence College, Bennington College, and New York University, spent the last 30-plus years of his career on the faculty at Claremont Graduate University. In 2002, he received the Presidential Medal of Freedom, the nation's highest civilian honor.

He died in November 2005, just shy of his ninety-sixth birthday.

Books by Peter F. Drucker

The End of Economic Man (1939)

The Future of Industrial Man (1942)

Concept of the Corporation (1946)

The New Society (1950)

The Practice of Management (1954)

America's Next Twenty Years (1957)

Landmarks of Tomorrow (1957)

Managing for Results (1964)

The Effective Executive (1966)

The Age of Discontinuity (1968)

Technology, Management and Society (1970)

The New Markets and Other Essays (1971)

Men, Ideas and Politics (1971)

Drucker on Management (1971)

Management: Tasks, Responsibilities, Practices (1973)

The Unseen Revolution (1976; reissued in 1996 under the title *The Pension Fund Revolution*)

People and Performance: The Best of Peter Drucker on Management (1977)

Adventures of a Bystander (1978)

Managing in Turbulent Times (1980)

Toward the Next Economics and Other Essays (1981)

The Changing World of the Executive (1982)

The Last of All Possible Worlds (1982)

The Temptation to Do Good (1984)

Innovation and Entrepreneurship (1985)

Frontiers of Management (1986)

The New Realities: in Government and Politics, in Economics and Business, in Society and World View (1989)

Managing the Nonprofit Organization: Principles and Practices (1990)

Managing for the Future (1992)

The Ecological Vision (1993)

Post-Capitalist Society (1993)

Managing in a Time of Great Change (1995)

Drucker on Asia: A Dialogue between Peter Drucker and Isao Nakauchi (1997)

Peter Drucker on the Profession of Management (1998)

Management Challenges for the 21st Century (1999)

The Essential Drucker (2001)

Managing in the Next Society (2002)

A Functioning Society (2002)

The Daily Drucker (2004, with Joseph A. Maciariello)

The Five Most Important Questions You Will Ever Ask About Your Organization (2008; posthumously released)

About the Drucker Institute

The Drucker Institute at Claremont Graduate University is a social enterprise whose purpose is to strengthen society by igniting effective, responsible, and joyful management. It does this by turning Peter Drucker's ideas and ideals into tools that are both practical and inspiring.

To meet its mission, the Institute hosts collaborative forums for executives from across all sectors; works with high school and middle school students to teach them basic management principles and equip them with lifelong tools for effectiveness; produces curricular material that distills Drucker's decades of leading-edge thinking, including a management training system called the Drucker Management Path; and acts as a hub for a worldwide network of Drucker societies: volunteer-driven organizations that are using Drucker's teachings to bring about positive change in their local communities.

In addition, the Institute maintains a digital archive of Drucker's papers and other holdings related to the fields of management and leadership; undertakes research that builds on Drucker's writings; offers an annual $100,000 prize for nonprofit innovation; applies Drucker's work to current events (through a regular online column in *Forbes* by Institute Executive Director Rick Wartzman; a daily blog called *The Drucker Exchange*; a monthly radio show called "Drucker on the Dial"; and hosts visiting fellows with Drucker-like insights and values.

The Institute is a close affiliate of the Peter F. Drucker and Masatoshi Ito Graduate School of Management, which is training the next generation of leaders and managers to do good while they do well. For more on the Drucker Institute, please visit druckerinstitute.com.

About the Authors

Rick Wartzman is the executive director of the Drucker Institute at Claremont Graduate University. He is also a columnist for *Forbes* online. Rick is the author of *What Would Drucker Do Now?*, a collection of his columns published by McGraw-Hill in 2012, and the editor of *The Drucker Lectures*, which McGraw-Hill published in 2010. Rick, who for 20 years was a reporter, editor, and columnist at the *Wall Street Journal* and *Los Angeles Times*, is also the author of two books of narrative history: *The King of California: J.G. Boswell and the Making of a Secret American Empire* and *Obscene in the Extreme: The Burning and Banning of John Steinbeck's The Grapes of Wrath*.

Anne Fishbein's solo and group exhibitions include the Los Angeles County Museum of Art, San Francisco Museum of Modern Art, Art Institute of Chicago, Track 16 Gallery, Blue Sky Gallery, Carnegie-Mellon University Art Gallery, El Motin de Los Angeles in Barcelona, and Lamont Gallery at the Mayer Art Center in Exeter, New Hampshire. Among the many museums and collections holding Anne's work are the Art Institute of Chicago, Museum of Modern Art in New York, National Gallery of Canada, Musee Niépce in France, and the San Francisco Museum of Modern Art. A book of her photographs from Russia, *On the Way Home*, was published in 2004.

Bridget Lawlor is the Drucker Institute's archivist. She received her M.A. in archival studies and history from Claremont Graduate University and is currently pursuing her doctorate there. Bridget recently served as an intern with the A. K. Smiley Public Library, where she worked with accessioned collections for Abraham Lincoln and the Civil War era. She is a recipient of CGU's Ida Lloyd Crotty fellowship, which supports an outstanding woman scholar in the arts or humanities.

Peter F. Drucker

P. S. Did I leave out anything important?

This is a note from Drucker to himself, found in a loose stack
of manuscript pages.